THE WILD LOVE OF GOD

CHRIS DUPRÉ

The Wild Love of God:
A Journey into Love that Heals Life's Deepest Wounds

Endorsements

—◈◈◈—

Wow! What a book. What a story. *The Wild Love of God* is a journey of radical forgiveness. In it Chris DuPré gives us his life message: the unconditional, healing, and transforming love of a loving heavenly Father.

Chris' personal transformation brought healing and life into the painful memories of his upbringing with his father, a former WWII POW. Reading this book is like watching a beautiful miracle unfold as deep healing first takes place in the son, and then transforms the heart of his father who needs forgiveness to have his own freedom.

I laughed and I wept as I read this wonderful gift to us all, *The Wild Love of God*.

BILL JOHNSON

Senior Pastor of Bethel Church in Redding, CA

Author of *When Heaven Invades Earth* and *Face to Face With God*

—◈◈◈—

In his book *The Wild Love of God*, Chris DuPré touches the hearts of us all. He tells a story of pain that we can all relate to and how forgiveness and the Father's love bring life and peace.

The Wild Love of God is a joyous read and a life-changing message!

JOHN ARNOTT

Founding Pastor of Catch the Fire Ministries

(Formally Toronto Airport Christian Fellowship)

—◦◦◦—

WITH GREAT JOY I WANT TO RECOMMEND TO YOU Chris Du-Pré's new book, *The Wild Love of God*. You are not just about to read a story of God's affection, you are about to find yourself in the middle of His gaze of love for you.

As a longtime friend, I know that Chris writes about what he knows. As you read his story, you too will begin to see the depth of God's heart for you. When you know His heart, it changes everything!

MIKE BICKLE

Founder and Director of the

International House of Prayer, Kansas City, MO

—◦◦◦—

LIKE A VOICE CRYING OUT IN THE WILDERNESS, my friend Chris DuPré brings us a treasure that releases relentless echoes of the Father's heartbeat right into the very essence of who you are as a person. Want to know the amazing love of God? Want to encounter

His persistent Presence? Do you need healing from a father-heart wound? Then this book was written with you in mind.

Chris' life message is contained in *The Wild Love of God*. The only thing it lacks is a warning label: "Warning: the contents of this book could change your life!"

With joy I highly commend to you this inspiring book, *The Wild Love of God*!

JAMES W. GOLL

Encounters Network | Prayer Storm | Compassion Acts

Author of *The Seer*, *The Lost Art of Intercession*,

The Coming Israel Awakening, and many more

CHRIS DUPRÉ'S BOOK *The Wild Love of God* is not your ordinary, run-of-the-mill Christian book. Rather, it is an eloquent and penetrating glimpse into the heart of a man who has found the depths of God's love in the midst of profound hardship.

I encourage you to read and ponder the life of my friend and his journey to become a friend of God. Chris' incredible story will pull you off the sideline of mediocrity onto the playing field of extraordinary adventures in God.

LARRY RANDOLPH

Author of *User Friendly Prophecy* and *Original Breath*

Dedication

I WANT TO DEDICATE THIS BOOK to David J. DuPré and Mary Kay DuPré, my father and mother. From two very different perspectives, you both showed me how deeply God loves. Dad, a man of deep emotions, you showed me the depths of His affection. Mom, a woman of valor and my hero, you unveiled to me over the years the steadfast love of the Lord. My love for both of you will never end.

Acknowledgements

Paul Rogers – Thank you, Paul, for believing that I not only had something to say, but you helped me get it out. You are a true friend and I thank God on a regular basis that you're in my life.

Renee DeLoriea – I could not have done this book without you. Your practical help and patience with me has been such a blessing. Laura and I are big fans!

Brad Cummings – My friend, you helped in more ways than I can say. Thank you for your generous heart and for the way you've helped me see Him more clearly. I look forward to walking together for a long time.

Carol DuPré – With eternal gratitude I thank you for leading me into the arms of God. You helped bring a family who thought they knew Him into the reality of being His friend. Love you, Carol Babe.

Mark DuPré – To my brother and my best friend, thank you for helping me sing. You gave me my voice. Even after all these years I still need to know your thoughts in a matter. You're a wise man and I'm honored to call you my brother and my friend. I love you.

Mike Bickle – My dear friend, Mike, thank you for helping to put more theology and a greater understanding to what I had already known and experienced concerning the depth of God's love.

You showed me the One Who sees the "Yes" in my heart and it's changed my life forever. I love you.

Andrea, Katie and Melissa – To be your father has been my joy and privilege. You've shown this dad how much it means to be loved by his children and in so doing, it has opened my eyes to understand how much my love means to Him. Your imprint is all through this book. I love you all so much!

Laura DuPré – You are the love of my life and I thank you for loving me back so well. We've had quite a journey so far and your love and support have been there throughout. You are beautiful inside and out. Everyone who knows you knows how much I married up. I love you, Laura DuPré! You are my greatest gift from God.

Contents

—⟨⟩—

FOREWORD BY MIKE BICKLE 13

CHAPTER 1: David's Story...................................21

CHAPTER 2: The Return of a War Hero 33

CHAPTER 3: In my Father's House...................45

CHAPTER 4: School Daze...................................55

CHAPTER 5: A New Song 65

CHAPTER 6: Face to Face 79

CHAPTER 7: Knowing the Father's Heart...................87

CHAPTER 8: The Journey of Forgiveness...................99

CHAPTER 9: The Gift of Forgiveness...................111

CHAPTER 10: Papa's Kiss...................................115

CHAPTER 11: The Gift Continues 131

CHAPTER 12: Wild Love...................................137

DISCUSSION GUIDE...................................147

Foreword

by Mike Bickle

—◦◦◦—

A HEART RAVISHED BY THE LOVE OF GOD becomes a force, both to love God and to love others. I've known Chris DuPré for twenty years and he is a man whose heart has been overwhelmed by the love of God. His understanding of the Father's heart has touched and transformed countless lives, mine included.

I first met Chris in the early 1990s when he and his precious family moved to Kansas City. As our new seventh grade teacher, he became my youngest son's first teacher outside the home. That first place of common ground brought us together as teachers, fathers, and friends.

Chris is a master storyteller. For years he has unveiled God's love through his anointed music, his teachings, and his life. Now (after my having encouraged him for years to do this) he has finally put his story and his revelation of God's great affection to pen and paper. What Chris has written will forever change the way you look into the eyes of God and understand how this same God sees you.

What makes this all work is knowing that Chris does not just write about God's heart, he also lives as one who releases the heart of God on a daily basis. I have not just looked into his eyes and found love there, I have witnessed time and again others who, in not knowing him, have approached him tentatively only to be enveloped in the Father's love through his smile, his kind eyes, and his warm embrace. He's the real thing.

The book you hold in your hands today is the result of not just hours of work, but of a lifetime of gathering. Chris has immersed himself in the Father's love so that others may know and experience that same great affection.

My heart is filled with joy over this book and I am certain that it will take you deeper into the river of God's love, making you lovesick for an even closer dance with Him.

MIKE BICKLE

Founder and Director of the

International House of Prayer, Kansas City, MO

I HAVE WANTED TO WRITE THIS BOOK for a long time. Not because I want to get *my* book out there, but because I wanted to get the knowledge of *His heart* out there. I've noticed over thirty-seven-plus years of ministry that people of all ages and types have a unique similarity: People struggle with knowing—really knowing—if God sees them and loves them just for who they are and not for what they do.

When I met the Lord in 1973, I felt like I had met this famous stranger in a dark alley and then, after meeting Him, I was instructed that my number-one duty in life is to love Him more. Through the years, I have been encouraged to love the Lord by hearing men teach, yell, weep, use humor, tell stories, tell longer stories, even rip phone books apart. Through a myriad of ways I have been told to love Him more. The problem is, I have rarely been told *how* to love Him more.

Try loving someone more because someone tells you that you *need* to love them more. It doesn't work. Try telling your kids to fall in love with the person you picked out for them instead of who they have already fallen in love with. You may grow in love over time, but telling someone to love more right now just does not work. All it does is leave the hearer with the idea that they are probably doing something wrong or that they have a deeper problem, a hard heart, that for some reason just doesn't love God to the same degree as those around them.

As lovers of Jesus, it should be our joy to not just remind people to love Him with all their hearts, but to give them a reason to fall more in love with Him. We need to unveil Him. We need to reveal His heart. When we do that, others can't help but fall more in love with Him.

I remember in fifth grade I had a crush on a girl named Pat. I wrote out an elaborate letter that went something like this: "Do you like me?" I know, amazing. Below that there were two boxes; one said, "Yes," and the other said, "No." Between them was written, "Check one." I was quite the romantic. I remember waiting for what seemed like an eternity for the answer to that note. It finally came. She did. Yeah! So, why was it so important? Why was I waiting on pins and needles for her answer. Because we all live for the answer to that question, "Do you like me?"

The most important question we can ever ask is, "Is there a God." Right on the heel of that question is, "So, how does this God feel about me?" Before we can really ask how we feel about God, we need to know how He feels about us. That's the correct progression. That's the question that determines how we live.

In Ephesians 4:13-14, Paul tells us that we all need to come to the knowledge of the Son of God so that we would no longer be children, tossed to and fro. The tendency of children is to follow. They are directed from the outside as opposed to being moved from within. Mature believers, however, are rooted and grounded in love, who can then go on the journey to be greater lovers of Him. If we are unsure of the knowledge of His heart, we will forever be trying to gain His favor, instead of living out of the knowledge of His favor.

Therefore, the question remains, "How does God see me?" When we answer that, we begin to walk out the rest of our lives.

I love how tender John the Apostle gets in his writings. He often addresses people as "little children" or just a simple, "Beloved." They are very tender and personal terms that help us get a handle on his heart. God then uses John's heart to speak to us about His own heart.

One of the simplest and most well-known verses is also, if we see it right, one of the most empowering verses in the entire Bible. In 1 John 4:19 we are told, "We love Him because He first loved us." Very simple and yes, very well known. Yet, it is the answer to the yearning in our hearts if we desire to love Him more.

We love *because*. That "because" is everything. If I were to rephrase it, it would sound something like this: "*Because* He loves us, we can love." Or how about, "We have the capacity to love *because* He first fills us with the understanding of His love for us." Or how about, "My ability to love is directly related to my ability to know how deeply I'm loved."

It reminds me of an old sixth-grade math class, the one with the bar graphs. If you were to put one bar out that was labeled, "How much I know I am loved by God," the bar that reads, "How much I love," can only be as long as the first, never longer. My ability to love is always contingent upon my ability to see and understand His love for me. I love *because*.

Why is that? Why do we have to know His heart before we can fully love Him back? Ask a farmer to grow anything without soil, rain, or sun. He'll look at you like you're crazy. You can take any seed, but without a place for it to be rooted, it will forever sit there only as incredible potential. You can yell at it, tell it how big other seeds have grown (guilt it into growing), or teach it how it's supposed to grow.

But in the end, it's fruitless, literally. Seeds are meant to be planted and rooted and so are we. We are meant to be planted in the truth of His Word and to be rooted in the knowledge of His love. We can learn the language of love over time and we can all learn to say the right things, but correct words can never replace loved hearts.

Recently I was at a church sharing about the healing power of God's love when we had a time of questions and answers. After a few questions were thrown at me, I asked one of the pastors a question: "What did the senior pastor preach on four weeks ago?" He stood there trying to connect with the message of four weeks earlier but could not.

Finally, after a couple of minutes, someone in the crowd came up with the answer and we all had a good laugh. I then asked him if he could tell me, from beginning to end, the story of *The Wizard of Oz*. He laughed and then proceeded to tell everyone the story in great detail. It was the *story* that he remembered, not the words to a sermon.

Statistics show that we retain only 7 percent of what we hear. Most of what people take away from a message or a person is not the words, but the impression made upon their minds and their hearts. Therefore, in order to share my heart "in words," I knew I had to do it through the story of my journey.

Not too long ago I ran into an old friend from my days in Kansas City. It was wonderful to see his face. We hugged, and as we did, he gave me a sweet kiss on the cheek, something not uncommon between us. As we sat and caught up on the time between our last visit, I was reminded of when I first met him and when I first grew to love him.

We were on the pastoral staff of a large church in Kansas City and we both were deeply involved in the lives of many people, thus making our lives very busy. We enjoyed each other but never got to really know each other well enough to feel great affection. He would probably say the same about me as I felt about him: "He's a great guy. Don't know him well, but I think I'd probably like him."

As time passed we found ourselves also being involved in the same ministry to young adults. Through this ministry, we were invited to come and speak to a group of young adults in Columbus, Ohio. Because of the number of kids that wanted to go from our church, we wouldn't be able to fly. We would instead have to drive.

We filled the van with kids and took off, the two of us up front. I was a bit nervous as I knew the trip was about twelve hours and I hoped we would have something to say for at least a chunk of that time. Otherwise, it was going to be a long trip.

We started out with the usual small talk, but after awhile, we began to ask each other questions about our lives. Soon we were deep in conversation about our journeys in life. I shared part of my story and then he shared part of his. We went back and forth, not just on the way to Columbus, but also on the way back home.

When we returned home, we both admitted that something had happened within each of us. Something unexpected. We no longer just enjoyed each other; there was now a new and profound love that we both felt for the other. In the telling of our stories, we saw the heart of the person, and in doing so, we fell in love with who that person was.

Knowing the myriad of books that focus on the love of God and that the Church is filled with many wonderful theologians, I chose to make this a book that unveils the affection of God through stories—stories that are familiar to me because they are stories that I have lived through.

Jesus chose to reveal Himself and His Father not just through His actions, but also within the words of parables…stories. He was a master storyteller and He wants to use the stories of our lives to tell the world of His great love and affection.

At the end of this book are some discussion questions for either individuals or groups. My prayer is that they would help steer you into a greater understanding of His heart and His ways. It's a worthwhile journey.

My prayer is that through this story you will fall in love again with the One who made you—the One who made you so that He could love you. There is only one you and His love for you is uniquely made with you in mind. That's why our stories are so important. Like a star, no two are the same. Therefore, within every God story is a new facet and unique perspective of God's nature and heart.

May you find His heart for you within my story, and through it, fall more in love with Him. The Wild Love of God awaits you. Enjoy the journey!

CHAPTER 1

David's Story

It was the summer of 1982. This year's Fourth of July gathering at my dad's house would be different. It had to be. I had something very specific to say to him. I didn't know how I would say it, I just knew this wasn't about me. This was about me giving my dad a gift, the gift of forgiveness. A gift that could have absolutely no strings attached.

Giving him this gift meant that I could not craft my words to manipulate the moment, at least not in a way that would give me the restoration moment that my heart needed so badly. It had to be unconditional.

Dad had always loved gardening, especially in his later years. It had become a point of contact for us (and for anyone else he could pull into the backyard to show off his garden). So, there we were, standing at the garden's edge, just twenty yards or so from the back deck. As we stood side by side, I sensed the Presence of Jesus. It felt like He was standing there with me. He was reminding me that I wasn't going to be doing this alone, and I needed to know that.

———

M Y DAD PROBABLY WOULD HAVE GONE TO COLLEGE right out of high school, but instead, like so many others during World War II, he lined up and joined the military. I could never figure out why he chose the Air Force, though. He was afraid of heights. He hated to fly. I laugh whenever I pull out one of the letters he wrote to my grandmother in 1944. I can almost see this skinny nineteen-year-old kid taking a gulp from a bottle of "pop," as he called it, while he wrote, "Gee, Mom, I've met some swell guys here." He actually did write that. He used the word *swell*.

He was in love with a girl back home. Her name was Mary Kay Murphy. In one of the letters to my grandmother he writes, "I hope to be a family someday, if Mary Kay will have me." "Mary Kay" would one day be my mom, but she hadn't yet given my dad much hope when he was writing those letters. Even so, he was already writing to her mother, Marjorie Murphy, and he was already calling her "Mom."

"God's Country" is what Dave DuPré called his place "back home." Thoughts of Ogdensburg, New York, a small town sitting along the St. Lawrence River, probably took him to what he loved most: fishing on his beloved river. There were pike and there were muskies, but how he loved fishing for those smallmouth bass. On those days, his dad, who could be hard on the boys, was jovial and carefree. "Hardworking and Irish Catholic" were the words people used most to describe his parents. The name DuPré was a little confusing to people at first, but the patriarchal family line was a long Irish one. Apparently, the name DuPré, which would usually signal French descent, had come in when a man married into the family in the mid-1800s, prior to a short-distance migration from Canada to upstate New York.

There were five DuPré kids: an oldest girl, my Aunt Jane, and then four boys. The boys were not only born close to each other, but were also as close as brothers could be. They had a saying between them that said it all: "If one of us has a dollar, we all have a quarter." They followed this motto throughout their lives. When the oldest brother graduated from high school, the younger ones got part-time jobs and helped put him through college. They then did the same for each other until all four brothers had graduated from college.

Pete, the oldest of the boys, had been the first to enlist. He was in the army, stationed in Europe. His brother Paul, just younger than my dad, was in the South Pacific. Before long, Paul would be the South Pacific's Marine Corps' gold-medal boxing champion of his weight class. Tom was too young to enlist, so he, along with Jane, would do their best to do what was necessary at home and not worry too much about their brothers.

I have a picture of my father from 1944, a young second lieutenant, completely out of step while he's leading a group of soldiers. A couple dozen young men were walking perfectly in unison with their right legs out while my dad proudly led them, his left leg sticking out like a sore thumb. He'd lost his step while the group was turning and the photo was snapped before he could get back into step with his men. His buddies put the picture up on the wall in the mess hall. You had to find fun somewhere.

Dad turned 20 in June 1944. With his chiseled face and square jaw, he looked like he could have played the dashing romantic lead in a classic 1940s movie. But this was no movie and dad had no time for romance. He had been trained to be a bombardier and assigned to the United States Eighth Air Force based in southern England. The B-17 crew he was a part of would fly from England, across the English Channel and be used in strategic bombing campaigns against industrial and military targets. They were mainly used to carpet bomb an area to create a path of lesser-resistance for Allied ground troops who were fighting their way east across occupied France and into Germany.

In his earliest missions he sighted targets and dropped bombs. The hundreds or even thousands of people who were injured or killed during those bombing runs would weigh heavily on him for years. I asked him when I was a little kid if he had ever killed anyone during the war. His face turned dark and he pulled back from me. He then said, "I was a bombardier. I'm sure I did." He turned and quickly walked away. I never pressed him again on that.

After his sixth mission or so he was sent back to the States to learn how to use this new thing called "radar," which made bombing, especially on cloudy days, much more effective. When he rejoined his B-17 crew, he was now the "radar man." In his new position, he was also responsible for the crew in the back of the plane. If anything happened, he would be in charge of making sure they got out, and the captain would work to get the crew in the front out.

He was on his thirteenth mission when new orders came over the radio. The squadron was to keep heading east, right into Western Germany. There appeared to be an opening into a specific portion of Western Germany. It was the beginning of 1945, and initial bombing runs into Germany were needed as the Allied Forces were pushing toward Berlin.

Unbeknownst to the B-17 squadrons, heavy German artillery guns positioned at the border were waiting for them. When the squadron crossed into Germany, my dad's B-17 shook violently as

Allied planes began exploding on all sides. The big guns below were swung into position to take down one Allied bomber after another.

Soon the sky was filled with enemy aircraft. Within a matter of minutes the quiet lull of plane engines sneaking into enemy territory had turned into absolute mayhem. Guns were going off. Planes were exploding. Smoke and flack filled the sky. My dad's plane was hit and the crew knew the plane would soon be going down.

When a B-17 was no longer able to function in formation, the pilot removed the plane from the group and tried to get away on its own. Usually that was the kiss of death. When my father's plane detached from the group, it was met by a hoard of German Messerschmitts, a small but effective fighter used by the Germans. My dad's plane didn't have a chance.

Knowing his time was short, my dad stood up to check on his best buddy, the plane's tail gunner. When he stood, a piece of shrapnel flew through the air, ripping through his mask and sticking it to the plane's inside wall. Had he been in any other position it would have gone through his head. He would later say that at that moment he felt like God had saved him.

Removing the rest of his shredded mask, he went to check on his friend. Upon seeing that his friend was heaped over, my father lifted him up to see how badly he had been hit. What he saw would be burned into his memory. His friend's head was almost completely severed from his torso.

Returning to the front of the plane, my dad saw the port gunner slumped over. My father realized his friend, a gentle young man, was unconscious but was unable to rouse him. Without hesitating, he held onto the gunner's ripcord while he pushed him out of the plane, and in so doing the parachute was released. Incredibly, he survived.

A couple of other men from his plane parachuted out until my father and the pilot were the only ones left on the plane. They gave each other a thumbs-up as if to say, "Everyone's taken care of on my end," and then they each jumped from the plane. Three seconds after my father jumped, the plane exploded. In a minute's time, God had saved my dad's life twice.

As my father was falling, an explosive wave thrust him backwards before gravity took its hold and plunged him into a rapid free-fall toward earth. When best to pull the ripcord was drilled into the men. Whenever planes would take off or land, the pilots would always yell out "1500." This was so the crew would look out the plane's windows to memorize what the 1500-foot elevation looked like. That way they would know the right time to pull the ripcord if indeed they ever did have to parachute. Injury or death from hitting the ground too hard would be there to greet you if you pulled the cord too late. If you pulled it too soon, though, you'd be an easy target for flying shrapnel or guns on the ground.

My dad dropped to what he thought was 1500 feet and went to pull the ripcord. Unfortunately, it was not in the right spot. He franticly searched for it and finally found it on the opposite side of where it should have been.

When he finally did pull the ripcord, he was in for quite a shock. He would later say that he learned a very valuable lesson that day: "Never, ever, under any circumstances, put your parachute on upside down."

The moment he pulled the ripcord his shoulder muscle tore away from his shoulder blade as his parachute violently whipped him around until his feet were above his head. In desperation, he fought through the pain while struggling to get his feet below his head before he hit the earth. When he finally pulled himself through the parachute cords, he saw wetlands were below him. He directed his chute toward a field, but when he had floated a little closer, he realized it was a cornfield. And not just any cornfield, a field of cut corn. Anyone who was raised in farm country would know that a field of cut corn is like a field of swords sticking straight up in the air. For a kid, the swords are to play with. For a man hanging from a parachute, the swords mean something very different.

Suddenly he spotted a small area where there was no corn. When he realized why it was free of corn (turns out corn doesn't grow on boulders), it was too late. All he could do was turn his body so that as little of it as possible smashed into the boulder. His right leg took the brunt of the impact and broke in nine places. Here he was, on the German side of the border, with muscle pulled away from his back, and his leg broken like an accordion. Knowing he needed to take cover, he dragged himself to a row of hedges nearby. He hunkered down in the middle of the bushes, laid his gun across his chest, and fell unconscious.

A young, teenage girl was kneeling over him and shaking him when he regained consciousness. He heard her voice before he was alert enough to do what comes naturally to a soldier who is startled out of unconsciousness. He admitted later that if it had been the enemy, he wouldn't have had the strength to even lift his gun, let alone fire it.

Out of the fog he heard her say, "Parlais vous Francais?"

A groggy, "No" was his answer.

She then said, "Sprechen Sie Deutche?"

"No," he said again.

Finally he heard, "Do you speak English?"

"Yes, yes," he replied and then again, quickly returned to his fog.

She left for a short time. He was greatly relieved when she came back with what looked like townspeople rather than the police or German soldiers. The men who carried him to a nearby farm told him they were part of the French underground. He was on the very edge of the Germany-France border.

These members of the French Resistance who were dedicated to sabotaging the Germans in every way possible did their best to treat his injuries, but they did not have the medications he needed. When they told him that if he didn't take antibiotics his leg would become gangrenous and have to be amputated, he agreed to be turned over to the Germans. The Germans had a reputation for respecting Allied officers enough to treat their injuries.

The Germans transported him to an old warehouse complex in Berlin where low-level medical professionals treated several hundred American and British officers. Looming in the air at all times was the fear that Allied forces might bomb the place at any moment because the building looked like a place where artillery and supplies were stored. In actuality, it was really nothing more than a warehouse. No signs or symbols had been put on top of the buildings to notify Allied bombers that the site was being used as a hospital. On the other hand, the locations where German military personnel were treated by the best physicians and nurses were clearly marked.

The buildings on the site formed the shape of an "H." My dad's room was in the lower right-hand leg of that H. His doctor told him, "Because you're an officer, we are taking good care of you. Then you will be transferred." In other words, they were getting him healthy enough so that he could then go to a German prison camp.

One night my dad was jarred out of his sleep by exploding bombs and buildings. He took cover as the wing that made up the middle portion of the "H" was completely bombed out and a large section of the building directly across from him was demolished.

The portion of the building where he was huddled shook wildly from the explosions. As dawn approached, he looked outside and saw the cause of what had suddenly made the ground erupt next to his room. An unexploded American bomb was embedded in the ground with its tail sticking up in the air just twenty yards outside his window. He felt that his life had been spared a third time. "Somehow, for some reason, God wants me to live," he thought. That confidence is what kept him going during the much harsher times ahead.

He knew he was alive for a reason and would one day go home to discover why God's protection had saved his life three times in what seemed like very miraculous ways. Back home his belief in God had been part of a camaraderie in his Catholic community. Church was a very important part of life. The family made sure to get the kids to Mass every Sunday. God was to be honored, as was the Church. Lying on that bed in the German hospital, his faith in God suddenly became much more personal.

When he was "healed enough," he was transferred to a Nazi prison camp. It was early 1945 and the war was ticking down. The Germans were desperate for military replacements for their dead and wounded soldiers. This meant that hotheaded twelve- to fifteen-year-old boys were given rifles to guard prisoners.

One young Nazi guard, who had probably been in the Nazi youth movement, had it in for my dad right away. He saw my dad as having been well taken care of in a hospital while Germans who were sick or injured were not receiving the treatment they needed. Slamming his rifle into my dad's head when the two passed in a corridor was just one of the ways he exacted his revenge.

The cell was dark and dank, making it hard to breathe. Every meal was just enough mush made out of grain, rutabaga, and water to keep a man alive. He later told me that things went on there that I just didn't need to know about. I tried to pry the information from him but I only received generalities.

He did say that only the German officers weren't abusive and that his comrades there were amazing men who all deserved the highest of honors. The only other thing he would always make mention of was that he never, ever wanted to eat another rutabaga.

As the Allies moved into the interior of Germany, my dad and the other prisoners were moved from one location to another. Some were old warehouses, others were just holes in the ground. The prisoners knew the war was coming to an end when the guards toned down their abuse. This often happens at the end of wars, when prison guards know that their prisoners may soon become their guards.

A small number of guards voiced thoughts of executing the prisoners in the final hours before the camp was abandoned, but that did not happen. Instead, General Patton and his troops liberated the camp and my dad was transported to a home that was being used to house recuperating ex-prisoners before going back home.

My Uncle Pete was stationed in Europe during this time and had only heard that my father was missing in action. No one knew if he was dead or alive. He was hoping but had little faith he'd ever see his brother Dave again. Having recently been promoted from Corporal to Sergeant, he was sitting at his desk, going over papers from his day's activities when the phone rang. He picked up the phone and said, "Hello." A voice answered and asked, "Is this Corporal DuPré?" My uncle, enjoying his new rank promptly corrected him, "No, this is Sergeant DuPré." The voice on the other end then said, "Well, this is Lieutenant DuPré."

Hesitating a few seconds to take it in, my uncle then replied, "Listen, I don't know who you are, but you need to know that's not funny at all!" Without missing a beat, my father quietly said, "Pete, it's Duke." With that, my father began his journey home.

The Return of a War Hero

As I stood next to my dad on the edge of the garden, I sensed God's Presence and knew this was the window of time for what I needed to say. I knew that just saying, "I forgive you" implied that there was something to forgive and might lead to a hostile response from him. For my gift to be unconditional, it would have to be given without being shaped by my fear of his reaction to my words.

Upon arriving at my dad's house earlier that day, I was looking for any indication as to how he might receive what I would soon be sharing. There was already a crowd at the house. Looking around for my dad, I saw him in the back yard eyeing his garden. As I stepped onto the back porch, he turned and we locked eyes. I saw nothing that would steer me in any direction, and so, I headed in his.

———❦———

DAVE DUPRÉ CAME HOME A WAR HERO. Everyone had thought he was dead, but he returned in uniform, on crutches, and with a full cast on his right leg. He looked so handsome in his uniform that "Mary Kay" took a second look at him. At every turn someone else was saying, "Mary Kay, you would be an idiot not to marry him. He's going to be a teacher here and come on, he's so handsome. You two would have such beautiful children together."

She didn't know yet that the "aw shucks" Dave that was "like family" before the war was now a little different. And she had no way of predicting that, before long, she would begin to see the two different Daves—the Dave before the war and the Dave after the war. So, when this war hero who had been a family friend for years asked her to marry him, she thought, "Well, my mom already loves him and this is what girls my age do, isn't it?"

A year after the wedding a baby girl came along. They named her Carol. She was a redhead with all that goes along with that. Cute, energetic, and full of spit and vinegar. As the oldest, she was the first to experience pain from the hands of my father. Six years later Mark was born. He had a blood disorder called purpura and was in the hospital a lot, particularly the first couple of years. He was physically weak and had to be watched over vigilantly. Dad really didn't know what to do with him, so he pulled back, physically and emotionally. A year later I was born, strong and healthy.

I didn't know that fathers were not supposed to hit their kids. I just assumed that a slap was a normal daily thing and that when he was really mad, well, anything was possible. I knew a couple of other kids who were also hit by their dads, so I just assumed it was the norm. I was wrong.

After going back to college to get his teaching certificate, Dad became a high school teacher. History was his love and so being a history teacher suited him well. He received teacher-of-the-year awards year after year.

When I started kindergarten, I was in the same K-12 school where he taught. I was so surprised by what I saw the first time I saw

him in his classroom that I stopped dead in my tracks. I ha~~
on my tiptoes to see through the window on the door. I'm s~~nd
mouth was hanging open and my eyes were bulging. I might ~~
even been shaking my head back and forth as I thought, "Who ~
this man? I don't know him."

He was sitting on the edge of his desk like he was just as comfortable and happy as could be. He was smiling and laughing, and those huge high school kids were smiling and laughing right back at him. I was even more shocked when I would be walking down the hall and one big kid after another would say to me in passing, "Hey, Mr. DuPré's your dad, right? Wow, he's my favorite teacher." It seemed like he was everybody's favorite teacher. At five years old, my little brain just couldn't get around it. This was not the man I knew! I had seen him acting all happy like that when we'd go fishing with his brothers, but this was with kids.

I had just started kindergarten the first time someone came to get me out of my class because my dad had called for me. Dad had taught me to recite the names of all of the U.S. presidents in order by the time I was four. At the start of every school year he would announce to his tenth-grade American History class, "Before the end of this month you will learn all of the presidents in order. This will give you an understanding of the continuity of the history of the United States so when you learn about the history of each president, you will know the history of the country."

Of course, every year the students would groan, "We have to learn *all* the presidents by the end of the month? That's just too hard!" He then walked over to the little telephone hanging on the his room. His mannerisms said, "Well, it's all of you who are ing me to do this," as he picked up the little phone and called y classroom.

"Your dad wants you," said my teacher.

Standing at about three-and-one-half feet tall, I felt very small in his big world called the high school wing. The hall behind me was empty, so my knock created an eerie echo. I heard my dad's voice from behind the big door, almost like he was a magician with something up his sleeve. He said, "Come on in."

The door creaked as I opened it. The rest of the room was silent. There my dad stood, all the way across the room, smiling an awfully big smile. I wasn't smiling, though. I stood frozen in the doorway.

"Chris, stand right here." His voice was unnaturally cheery. I moved in cautiously to the spot he was pointing to. It was dead center, right up in front of thirty or so kids who were taller than I, even though they were sitting down.

"Chris, say the names of the presidents—in order, of course."

I named them, George Washington straight through to Dwight D. Eisenhower. It *was* 1959.

"Thank you, Chris, you can go back to your *kindergarten* class now." The emphasis on "kindergarten" made me think that he was proud that I could name the presidents even though I was only in kindergarten. I thought he was so proud of me that he wanted his whole class to know that his son, who was just a kindergartener, could do something that other kindergartners couldn't do.

I didn't know why the kids burst into moans and groans as I left the room. I had no idea that my dad had just made a point that their complaints of it being too hard did not hold any water and would not get them out of the "kindergarten level" memory work.

The call for me came two more times that week as my dad had three tenth-grade American History classes each year. I thought my time to shine had really come because my dad was finally so proud of me.

I didn't understand why his students suddenly stopped being nice to me in the halls and started poking me or hitting me with their books when they saw me. It would be a couple of years before I figured out that he was using a five-year-old to show them up and prove his point.

I was in the second grade when I looked at my dad and saw that it wasn't me that he was proud of. He was proud of himself. That was the last time I recited the presidents in his class. When the call came for me to do it again, I made up an excuse like I didn't feel well. When I had been in kindergarten and in the first grade, I was convinced that he was so proud of me. But now that I was seven, I wasn't sure anymore. I now thought he was proud of himself and his ability to teach me to do it. And so as a result, I felt used. I felt like he was setting himself up to look good through me. And without knowing it, he was also setting me up to make the other kids not like me.

By this time I was no longer confused by the difference between the man at home and the man at school. I figured the one at home hit me with his hands and the other hit me with the smile on his face. At age seven I was stronger and more physically active than my brother, so I was his constant target now that my sister Carol was a teenager.

My dad's leg and back had healed up, but the way he handled stress was another story. People didn't talk about post-traumatic stress syndrome back then. I'd never even heard the words. My dad was stuffing what had happened to him just like he was stuffing other things he didn't want to deal with—like household bills.

Mom was always finding unopened bills in the back of his drawers or stuffed in a shoebox on the floor or the top shelf of his closet. He was so overtaken with fear when he looked at a bill that he just wouldn't pay it. That's when he would come looking for me.

That's also why we'd have to move from place to place. By the time I was eight we had moved into nine different homes. I stopped putting my clothes in my dresser. I would just lay them over my bed or a chair. I just thought, "Why bother, we'll be moving soon."

He was verbally abusive almost all of the time, and I was always on the lookout for signs that physical abuse was coming. I knew I really needed to watch out if I heard him slam his car door a certain way. I would start listening for that sound when it started getting close to the time he would be getting home from work. If the slam was abrupt and hard, I did my best to avoid him.

If I heard him walking down the hall, I would stay in my room and hide until I heard him in another part of the house. The last thing I wanted to do was end up passing him in the hall where he could get an easy whack at me. He seemed to enjoy smacking us kids in the back of the head for no reason. Predicting his behavior wasn't always possible, though.

Sometimes life seemed to be going along okay but then things would suddenly shift. This kept me constantly on edge because I didn't know if I would be hit or just yelled at if I said something in a way he didn't like or asked him a question he didn't want to answer. Over and over I'd let my guard down just a little bit because I was hoping for a little bit of normalcy, but then, boom, he'd turn on me again.

My many lessons in the basics of physics—force, speed, and velocity—began when I was four years old. I learned that when a grown man forcefully pushes you away, you first hit the floor really hard and then you slide with great speed across the room until you come to an abrupt stop when you hit the wall.

The bruises from where he had hit me blended right in with the bruises from where I had collided with the ground while I was playing or with the branches while I was climbing trees. This made it easy for me to cover up the origin of the bruises when people asked questions.

One time in particular I had to work extra hard at covering up where I had gotten a large bruise from him. At the time we were living in what we called "the old stone fort," an old house made of stone with barely any insulation. It was always so very cold there. Dad would often forget to pay the bills and before going to bed we'd put on as many clothes as possible before bundling up in blankets.

When Mom asked me about my bruises, I mixed truth with fiction. The box in which I had slid down a hill with our dog Prince had hit a bunch of rocks. I knew the bruises she was asking me about really weren't from my box-sled ride with our big German Shepherd, but I presented her with a very convincing case. She could see the rocks in the snow, and the box had pretty much fallen apart by that time, so she believed my story.

I'm really not sure how much Mom knew about Dad hitting me. She laid into him right in front of me the one time I know for sure that she had seen him hit me. I was six or seven at the time when he gave me a side whack in front of her. She intervened on other occasions as well, backing him off when it was obvious that he was on the verge of hitting me.

There is a big difference between discipline and violence. What I received was not a father guiding his son or even spanking him because he did something wrong. It was not born out of love, and it was not connected to misbehavior on my part. For him, it was a violent eruption of pent up stress and emotion. For me, it was a life of regular verbal abuse, walking on eggshells, getting whacked randomly (but not all the time), and being hit severely every once in a while.

There were good moments here and there—I don't want to paint a picture that things were always horrible—but I was always on edge and on constant lookout for where his hands were when I was around him. My parents did not fight with each other. Their polite existence in the same household was very business-like. At the time I didn't think it was unusual that I never saw them kiss or hug. I didn't know any better. When I was older, I would learn that they had been separated two or three times before I was even conceived.

They might have been together out of Catholic obligation. My mother was in charge of teaching catechism to the senior high, my dad was one of the readers and took the offering, my sister was in the choir, I was an altar boy, and my brother played the organ for the choir. We were committed, that's for sure.

We were also in survival mode, moving from house to house, and it was easy to see that Mom's patience with the situation was wearing thin. Rather than trying to explain what was going on with Dad, she would encourage me by saying things like, "It's not always going to be like this," and "We are going to be okay."

My mother was an amazing woman. During the war she went into the WAC (Women's Army Corps) and learned how to fly. She was such a good pilot that she became a top flight instructor at the military base. This same incredible woman was then suddenly reassigned to secretarial duties when some insecure military leader determined that "women shouldn't be training men to fly."

She made it a point to convey to me in numerous ways, "I will find a way to make a better life for you." I had seen pictures of her dressed in a pilot's uniform standing next to planes. I knew there was more to her than being the quietly oppressed wife and mother. At one time she had been very independent, but now, she appeared to be overtaken by a man who had a great weakness in him because of what the war had done to him.

The change came when I was eight. It was the summer of 1962.

We had made a safe landing at my grandmother's house in downtown Rochester, New York, after again being forced to leave a place we had called home for a very short time. One day after shopping, Mom walked in the back door at the exact moment my dad knocked me off of my feet and I went flying into a wall. As I tried to catch my breath, I looked into my mother's eyes and she looked back at me in a way that said, "I am here to protect you."

Shortly after that, we all vacationed back at the St. Lawrence River. It was not a two-week stay this time. It was the whole summer and my mother, who didn't always do the River trips, was there.

Everyone seemed to be on edge. We had fun with our cousins but things felt very different. It turned out that during this time, my mother was planning our departure when the summer was over. At the end of our time on the river, Dad headed back to Rochester and we headed to Marion, thirty miles away.

I do realize that our move to Marion was a much bigger issue than what I had been going through. I was just one small piece of a larger picture. My parents had gone through a number of separations before this one. It just seemed to me, at the tender age of eight, that my mother had somehow ridden in on a white horse and saved the day. She did what was needed for us and for herself. We moved and I felt safe for the first time.

Every day was the same in our tiny house that Mom set up for us in the small town of Marion, New York. Things were stable and peaceful. Mom was always in the kitchen when I came home after school. We played games or sat on the couch and watched movies together. Of course, we brothers fought like all brothers do and I thought my sister was a stupid teenager, but we were safe. Life had an easy and normal flow. I knew what to expect and could finally rest and relax in my own home.

Until he was able to secure his own apartment, Dad stayed at my mom's mother's house. Manu, as we called her, remembered what he was like before the war and wanted to do what she could to help him. Without family responsibilities weighing heavily on him, he was now free to become a great teacher, and because of the routine, he could now handle the administrative side of teaching. With us, though, whenever he would see us, depending upon his mood, he was either surly or uncomfortably nice. We never knew what to expect.

In my
Father's House

The happy voices and laughter of our loved ones chatting and cutting up behind us on the back deck gave me some reassurance that my dad wouldn't hit me upside the head when I said what I was about to say. As a child I had always paid close attention to where his hands were. Now, here I was, a grown man with a wife and children of my own, and yet I was still paying attention to every movement of his hands. I was still in hyper-alert mode, ready to duck or back away if need be, even though he was entering the backside of middle age and I was in my prime.

The risk that afternoon wasn't, in reality, a physical one. I knew that. The possibility of him verbally exploding, though, loomed large. Although our relationship only ran as deep as the reciting of current events in our lives, it was something I valued greatly and didn't want to lose. Contemplating the possible loss of this fragile connection to my father brought back memories of a time when I was much younger and had taken a similar risk.

———

WHEN I WAS IN HIGH SCHOOL, my only real connection point with my dad was sports. The field and the bleachers were far from one another, but at least it was something. I fell into this performer/viewer relationship with him for a lot of reasons. For one thing, I was naturally athletic and sports came easily for me. Also, I had seen my parents dote on a teenage boy who lived with us for a few years.

He moved in when he was around sixteen and I was four or five. During the time when my parents were having so many marriage problems, they brought in Jake and another teenager, Owen, as foster brothers. Our family was falling apart, so maybe they thought that helping two boys whose own lives and families were also falling apart would somehow help us.

Owen caused some havoc in our home before going into the Navy, but Jake, well… Jake was my hero. In fact, he was the king of our home and the king of our town. Small towns do that to sports heroes. During this time, my mom became Jake's second mother and my dad treated him with kid gloves. Seeing him get the royal treatment while my dad treated the rest of us so abrasively made me feel horrible. I loved Jake anyway, though. He let me come into his room anytime. He'd tell me about his day at school and describe in detail one of the many shots he'd made to win a game. Having the town basketball superstar living in my house and treating me like his kid brother sometimes seemed like I was living in a dream.

Loving and looking up to this larger-than-life figure made it harder and harder for me to endear myself to my dad. Not only was he treating his own children completely different than Jake, but the way Jake treated me so well seemed to throw a spotlight on how poorly my own dad was treating me. Jake became so important to me that after not seeing him for almost ten years, I broke down when I saw his silhouette in the door of the church on the day of my wedding. The sun was behind him and I couldn't see his face at all, but I knew it was Jake. I ran straight into his arms and began to weep. I hadn't seen him in years but his presence at my wedding meant everything to me. We just never know the impact we're having on others. Jake was one of the men that God brought into my life along the way who helped me to see that not all men are untrustworthy. He had his shortcomings, but he loved me well.

Before I was old enough to be in school sports, Dad would come over to the house on Sundays. I would have to stay indoors with him even though all he usually did was watch Cleveland Brown's football or Yankee baseball. My friends would be outside playing, but there I was, Sunday after Sunday, stuck inside, sitting on the living room floor, while my dad was sprawled out on the couch sleeping. I was the youngest, so unlike my brother and sister, I couldn't jump in the car and take off or come up with any good excuses for not hanging out with Dad.

I would sometimes see a great and wonderful man in my dad when we would go with him to the St. Lawrence River during the summer. He loved being with his brothers and their families. I would fish with my friends and my cousins, and on occasion he would be just like a regular dad for an entire day. In fact, anytime we'd spend a whole day with one or more of his brothers, I would see a gem of a man all day long. During those times I would see why the kids at school loved him. I would see the greatness of this man, but then suddenly it was gone when we were back behind the four walls of the house. I had no way of understanding back then that in many ways he was still in that prison camp—and we were there with him.

My senior year was supposed to be my sports glory year, which is the case for all high school athletes. However, that was not to be the case for me. The year before, as a junior, I was seated first in my district (Section Five) as the top triple jumper. The sectionals were in a small town in southern New York called Hornell. I was also seated first in the 440, a race that's one lap, or 440 yards. Now it's called the 400, as in the 400-meter race.

It was May of 1971. I was expected to easily win both events that day, which would qualify me for the state meet near New York City. Always keeping an eye on the other New York track athletes, I knew my times and distances were equal to or better than the others. That would mean, if things went according to plan, I would be going to the Nationals.

A lot was riding on this track meet. I had received letters from two of the top track schools in the country. There was a good chance that William and Mary and/or Villanova College would offer me a partial or possibly even a full-ride scholarship—tuition, books, and housing—if I stayed healthy and my track career continued to do well.

I was very excited that day because I didn't think anyone competing could beat me in either event. It wasn't a pride thing; it's just what the numbers said. I easily won the first 440, which qualified me to run in the finals later that day. I watched the other qualifiers run and the closest time to mine was about five seconds slower, which is forever in a race like the 440. After the qualifying races were done, I went over to the triple jump pit to get my mark and do some practice jumps for that event. Something about the pit looked wrong. I took out my tape and measured. Sure enough, it was not long enough from the take-off board to the end of the pit.

I realized that I would probably jump over the pit (I'd done that once at another pit) if I took off from the spot the other competitors were jumping from. So I asked one of the officials if I could move my take-off spot back. They hadn't expected anyone to be able to jump that distance, but they agreed and moved my jump-off point back so I would end my jump inside the pit.

When they cleared me for my practice jump, I had assumed that they had raked the pit. They had assumed that no one would land in the back of the pit. Well, I did. It was a great jump. I went almost 48 feet, a foot longer than my best jump. What happened next changed my life. Every tendon and ligament in my left ankle burst as my left foot landed on a rock that was hidden under a thin layer of sand. My ankle turned and twisted and popped so loudly that my coach heard it from over 100 yards away. When he saw me lying on the ground in pain, he ran to me as fast as he could. He asked me if I was OK and if I thought I could still run. I lifted my foot and we both knew the answer. My ankle was the size of a football. We both knew that I was finished, not just for the day, but for the season.

I could see by the look on my dad's face that he felt badly for me. He hurried over to me, but there was nothing he could do to change what had happened. I was rushed to a local hospital to get x-rayed. I was told that no bones were broken but the soft tissue around my ankle was shredded. The doctor actually told me that it would have been better if it was a broken bone, as the damage I now had would hinder me from ever having a strong ankle again. He said my jumping days were over. He put me in a soft cast, gave me crutches, and sent me home. Track scouts were in the stands, but I never heard from anyone again about a scholarship.

The injury was life changing in a number of ways. My ankle did get better, but because of the extent of the damage, (the doctor was right) I would never be able to triple jump again.

Another unexpected change launched me into new waters. My dad came over on one of his Sundays with a gift. He had a guitar. He figured I needed something to do while my ankle was wrapped and I had to spend a lot of time sitting at home on the couch. That "Kmart special" guitar was very light and much smaller than most guitars. However, it would bring me to a place where I would take the risk of being hurt by my dad in a different way in my search for a new connection point with him. It would also open the door to a world of music, and one day, to a life of ministry that I never even knew existed.

While I was teaching myself to play the guitar, I wrote a song about my dad. The idea of playing that song for him seemed like an awfully big risk because I felt there was a good chance he might get very mad when he heard it. Because I loved the Beatles so much, I'm sure he thought I'd only been playing their songs.

After my parents split up in the summer of 1962, we moved into a tiny but lovable house. At age eight I had begun having terrible temper tantrums. My mother was becoming very concerned. Also, for the first time in my life, I was struggling in school.

Then suddenly, the Beatles came on the scene. Their infectious music was upbeat and fun. I couldn't get enough of it. It had an effect on my soul—so much so that when I was nine, I formed a pretend Beatles band with my brother and two of my friends, who were twins. We made cutout guitars, put strings on them, and dressed up like the Beatles. I was John Lennon, Ricky was Paul McCartney, and Randy was George Harrison. My brother Mark would be Ringo. We'd put the speakers from the record player out on the porch and blast Beatle's music while we stood on the front lawn and mouthed the words to the songs. We put on quite a lip-syncing, fake-guitar show for people who were driving or walking by the house. My mother used to tell me, "The Beatles helped save your soul. They gave you your heart back." It was true. I suddenly had an interest in music that I'd never had. Much to the chagrin of my friends, I would sing everywhere I went.

When my dad bought me that guitar he might have been thinking that since Beatles music helped me so much when I was little, maybe eight years later it would help me again.

"So, have you been learning some Beatles songs?" he asked.

"Well, actually I've only been playing songs I wrote."

"Oh, play one of those then," he replied.

"Well, I wrote one based off the title of this book. I showed him the book. The title was, *In My Father's House*.

"It's about a guy who lives alone," I added. Here I was, sixteen years old. Seeing a book titled *In My Father's House* had made me think about what it must be like in my dad's apartment, a quiet place with no one there to say, "I love you." From there I had written the song with the same title. I had put this moment off for months.

After a long and uncomfortable hesitation, my dad finally spoke, "Okay, let me hear it."

"Well, here goes," I thought.

I fully expected him to explode at me, but instead, as I played the song, its haunting melody a backdrop for those intimate words, tears filled his eyes. When the song ended, he said nothing. Instead, he got up and left the room. I was devastated. I watched him leave not just the room, but he left the house. Looking through the window I saw him head straight for his car. As he opened his car door I turned away. Though I was sad and disappointed, I was also relieved that at least he hadn't exploded.

A minute later the front door opened and he walked back into the house. I was more than a little surprised. He had a serious and determined look on his face as he came back into the living room and headed straight for me. I noticed that there was something in his hands. It took me a moment to recognize it but when I did I caught my breath. Held between his big strong fingers was a small, black tape recorder. He said, "Would you sing it one more time so I'll always have it with me?"

Trying to hide my watery eyes, I put my head down and pretended I was tuning a string. After a pause I quietly said, "Okay." He then held a little plastic microphone up to my mouth as I went through it one more time. It was the longest few minutes of my life. I couldn't look at him as I sang it, but when it was over, he was crying again.

We now had a new connection point, one that took us beyond sports. Through that simple song, I told him that I saw his pain and cared about it. I had given him a glimpse of the real me, the young man who was more than just an athlete, and he hadn't rejected me.

Even though my dad told me that he'd played the song a couple of times for other people, I was really shocked some time later when my uncle Pete told me, "Yeah, your dad cries when he's driving around listening to that song." I had not seen that side of my dad, and so I was also really puzzled, yet deeply touched when my Uncle Pete added, "I had to listen to that song over and over again while I drove with your dad all the way up to the river."

Years later, I would learn that during this time of his life, he had been meeting with an older war veteran, who, now as a professional counselor, was helping my father talk through what had happened to him in the war. At the same time my life was taking a turn that would eventually lead to ministering to others, my dad was getting the help he needed that would eventually lead to his helping other veterans.

My dad's reaction should have told me that something was changing in him, but unforgiveness is a demanding boss. Because I was still blinded by my own pain and lingering bitterness, I couldn't yet see the man that others saw.

School Daze

Like a man facing potential death who sees his life flash before his eyes, I found myself filled with so many thoughts as I stood next to my dad. Okay, so it wasn't quite that dramatic, but I knew this was a pivotal moment. As we both gazed on the beauty of his garden, I knew one thing: in just a few minutes, things would be different, one way or another.

I WAS GLUED TO THE OLYMPICS whenever they were on TV. Like millions of kids, one of my dreams was to compete at that level. To get any kind of medal would be amazing, but just to be a part of something so wonderful would have been a dream. That dream was shattered in that triple jump pit along with my ankle. Both colleges had been looking for someone who could excel in very specific events in which I could now no longer compete. The events in which I could do well were areas where other athletes on their teams were already excelling.

Even after my injury I kept up hope, banking on the possibility that another school might offer me an athletic scholarship in track or soccer. I had relied on getting an athletic scholarship so much that I had ignored the obvious: school work.

I do not say this proudly, but I brought no homework home the last two years of high school. I told my mother that I had two study halls at the end of every day so I never needed to bring any work home. That was partially true because I often would do a little homework during athletic study hall before practice and do the rest during announcements and attendance time in homeroom the next morning. I could knock out a two-page book report in a 12-minute homeroom. Because I was good at stories, I only needed to scan a book to do a halfway decent book report on it. I didn't realize at the time that if I would have just studied, even a little bit, I probably could have earned an academic scholarship.

"Labeling" had blinded me from being able to see that my brother, whose IQ was at genius level and actually only a few points higher than mine, wasn't the only "smart one" and that my sister, who could hold a crowd's attention, wasn't the only "good communicator." I knew I was a smart kid and I knew I had good communication skills, but the "athletic one" label had given me permission to hide my insecurities in the shadows of my physical abilities, which kept me from developing my God-given potential in other areas. I never even thought about the possibility of any kind of scholarship except for an athletic one.

Depression did not fully set up shop in me during my senior year in high school because my ankle was able to recover enough, so that if I taped it every day, I could still play soccer. As captain of our team, we won the sectionals that year. Winning gave me enough of an adrenaline rush to keep me from nose-diving into a state of depression. I ended up making the first string all-county team. My hopes were high that some college would hear something about how I was doing. "Hey, I'm still here!" I was confident that since they had known me from track, surely they would notice what I was doing on the soccer field. They didn't.

While growing up, I had always played basketball every year. That's what you did during the winter in small towns, especially in small towns like Marion. It seemed like everyone from town would show up and pack the gym for every home game. It was so intense that one man actually had a heart attack during one of the games and had to get permission from his doctor to go back to the gym later in the season. Marion, a town of only four thousand, had that small-town atmosphere where people were nice to you when the team won but were rude or indifferent to you if you lost. When we won, we won as a town. When we lost, the players lost.

I'd had enough of that and thought that I really didn't enjoy basketball enough to bother with that kind of duplicity. I was a soccer and track guy. I did basketball because, unless you were into wrestling, that's what my friends and I had always done. There weren't many options.

A few of us decided that we would create another option. Since our school didn't have a volleyball team at the time, several of my friends and I decided to launch one ourselves. We were all tired of the small town basketball culture and determined that we would play volleyball instead and enjoy our last year of high school. Our German teacher had been on the German national volleyball team and volunteered to be our coach.

Needless to say, that did not go down well with the basketball coach. He called me into his office one day and asked me why I wasn't playing basketball. I told him that basketball was never my great love and that I was tired of the pressure brought by basketball season in a small town. I didn't mind competition or pressure. I had plenty of both with soccer and track. I just didn't like basketball all that much. It was my senior year and I wanted to enjoy it.

Suddenly, this 6'5" man, who had been coaching for years, stood up from behind his desk, walked directly in front of my chair, gave me a long intimidating gaze, and then slapped me across the face. The blow seemed to come out of nowhere. It was so hard that it knocked me off the chair.

I pulled myself up off the floor and sat back down, stunned at what had just happened. He then started yelling at me about how much talent I had and how I was wasting it. He added that I was influencing others to also waste their talents for a stupid sport like volleyball.

He said, "I was brought to this town to raise up a winning basketball team and you're working real hard to destroy that possibility." I looked back at him as if to say, "And this is the way that you're inviting me back to your team?" But instead I just said, "Are we done?" As he turned away he said, "Yes." I got up and headed for the door. I walked out of there with a big red hand-shaped mark on my face. Some of my friends asked what had happened to me, but I just said it came from a wayward blow from a bad rebound during gym class.

Back then, people didn't think about suing like they do now, and I wasn't going to report him to the principal. I had already learned to cover for my dad and so covering for him was the natural thing for me to do. My closest friends, whom I did tell later, didn't report him for what he'd done to me either. I understood…they were on the basketball team.

So for me, here was another man in a long line of authority figures who showed me that this is what will happen to you if you don't do what they want. My response to his physical and verbal slap was that I pushed ahead and played volleyball with everything I had. Our volleyball team ended up going to the sectionals. We didn't win, but boy, did we have fun.

My last sport of that year was again track. I didn't go into a funk because I knew I could still run fast. I knew I'd be winning races so I still held out hope. Halfway through the season, my coach decided to take one of our practices and use it as if it were a track meet. He even had his starting gun with him. He told us we could try any event we wanted. I decided to try the low hurdles. I had run them once as a freshman and had enjoyed it.

I got into the blocks for the start. The coach was at the finish line with his stopwatch and the assistant coach was our starter. When the gun went off, I took off. Our team's hurdler at the time was next to me. He was the No. 3 hurdler in the county and a solid athlete, but after the first hurdle I never saw him again. I crossed the line and my coach let out a shout. I ran over to him and he held out the clock. I asked him if it was a good time. He looked at me and said, "You just shattered the county record."

We both decided at that moment I would now also run the hurdles. It was already halfway through track season, but I ended up breaking not only the county record but also the sectional record.

Maybe now some college would come running. Maybe now I would hear from someone.

The local paper in Rochester did a small article about me and someone from Sports Illustrated contacted my coach about my possibly being in their youth section, "Faces in the Crowd." I waited, my coach made some follow-up calls, but nothing. Again, no colleges responded. I was devastated. I was a seventeen-year-old kid whose every track meet ended with people crowding around, some even asking for autographs. I thought for sure that I was going to hear from someone, anyone.

Looking back on it now, I know that God was in the midst of it all, but I didn't see it then. At the end of my senior year, all of my friends were heading off to college. My best friend Tom was headed to Cornell, another close friend had an athletic scholarship to Bucknell, and my brother was going back to Holy Cross for his sophomore year. It had seemed that at one time I'd had a scholarship and a future. Now I felt very empty handed. Everyone else had somewhere to go. It seemed as if I was going nowhere.

So there I was, or so I thought, in the race of sibling life, even farther behind my sister—Miss Comedy, and my brother—Mr. Academics. I had gone from being quite possibly one of the most confident sixteen-year-olds around to being increasingly afraid of an uncertain future. I was no longer able to compete athletically at the level I had been relying upon for my sense of security, social identity, and future success. It was killing me inside. Fear and deep sadness were welling up in me as it looked more and more like my future had also been shredded on a rock in that track pit. Of course, I kept all my feelings to myself and continued to walk out my life silently suffering from constant migraine headaches. I saw no connection between the two.

It never crossed my mind to look to God for help, comfort, or answers. I saw God as being a Judge who barely tolerated my existence. I figured I was on my own and God's hell-fire judgment was kept at bay through my weekly church rituals. I had never heard that you could have a personal relationship with God the Father through belief in His Son Jesus. I really didn't even know why Jesus died. The gist of what I had gathered from catechism, Scripture that was read on Sunday mornings, and comments I'd heard here and there was that Jesus died on a cross because of my sins and the church rituals would keep me from going to hell. I had no idea that Jesus ever thought about me and actually loved me. It had never entered my mind that He wanted me to be able to have a close, intimate, and personal relationship with Him, with God the Father, and with the Holy Spirit. I didn't realize that He had died for me so that He could give me a new heart. Instead of being secure in His affection, I was chasing after His approval and the approval of others.

It was nearing the end of the Vietnam War and so I, and most of the other guys around me who were graduating from high school, wanted to go to college so that we wouldn't be drafted into the war. Because my focus had totally been on sports, I did not look into other types of financial help that would have made my going to a four-year college possible. So after graduation, I literally went along for the ride when my friend Mike asked me if I wanted to go with him to a community college that was an hour away from home. I said, "Why not," and together we took off to a small two-year school in Auburn, New York. At least I'd have something to do. It was better than going to Vietnam.

Even though I was now starting for the college soccer team, my athletic goal had been kicked to the curb. In the past I had stayed away from drugs and alcohol so I could stay fit and reach my athletic goal. With that motivation gone, I saw no reason to avoid that lifestyle. I just didn't care anymore.

Though I still loved the game, by the time soccer season was over, I was drinking and doing drugs pretty much every day. A new friend named Bruce and I made a bizarre pact that we would get stoned sometime before the end of each day. In our "freedom," we would not let a day go by without getting wasted in some way.

It was my freshman year in college and depression had sealed me in with my new best friend—drugs. I only lasted one year at college before I quit school altogether. I was so spaced out that at the end of an entire year of school I had earned only twelve credit hours...for the whole year! I was often high when I was in class, and then had even more of a buzz when I was studying, which wasn't very often. It was so bad on some days that I couldn't even remember what classes I had just taken hours earlier.

I would often sign up for a class and then drop out because I just couldn't handle it. At the end of the year I told my mom, "I just can't do school now. I don't know what I'm going to do, but I just can't do school." She could easily see that I was in no shape to continue as I was. When the school year ended, I packed my bags and headed home. To me it signified another failure, confirming what I already felt: I was going nowhere.

Moving back home turned out to be a good move on many levels. The pressure I had to party every day while at school was replaced by the normal ebb and flow of daily life at home. I continued to do drugs, but now it was just a couple of times a week instead of every day. Hiding my drug use from my mother forced me to curb the amount I used as well as how often. At the same time, a close friend of mine had asked me to help her out with her family's dairy business. Nancy had been in my high school class and her dad could no longer drive. They needed someone to bottle the milk two days a week and do deliveries the other three days of the week.

There's nothing like starting work at 4 a.m. to help you curb your drug use, not to mention all of the appreciation Nancy's family showed me. Each work day that summer ended with the family preparing a feast for me while I lounged around their pool. It seemed they were not just saying thanks; they were celebrating my helping them at a time of crisis. Instead of frying my brains trying to feel good, I was actually doing something good for this family and providing a service to the community.

During that summer of 1973, the drug-induced cobwebs of the past year were clearing out of my head and at the same time like dominoes, my sister, my mother, my aunt, and finally my brother all received Jesus into their lives. Everyone at my house, even our neighbor, became born-again, all by the beginning of that summer. Everyone but me, that is. Outwardly, I joked about it. I even said that our cat was now probably saved. (The cat did seem different.) Inwardly, though, I halfway paid attention to what they were now saying, but I gave full attention to how they were now living.

A New Song

Standing there next to my dad, my heart was warm toward him and God's peace washed over me each time thoughts popped into my head like, "The last thing he wants you to do is bring up what happened in the past. Just be satisfied with what you have right now." Or, "You know how angry he can get. He might make a scene in front of all the family. And what about Marian and her kids? They'll all blame you for ruining such a nice day."

I focused on God's Presence at that moment rather than on past fears that would have held me back. My being able to feel God's Presence seemed to be God's way of letting me know that this was the moment that He had been preparing me for, step by step, year by year. In this moment of peace, I knew that all I had to do was open my mouth and God would fill it with just the right words.

This was not about performance or about managing my dad's reactions for me or for other people. I knew that the gift that I was about to give to my father had been born out of God's gift to me.

———

MY SISTER HAD NATURALLY CURLY, RED HAIR, and in 1973, she puffed it out into an Afro that was so monstrous, that, as I loved to joke, she had to turn sideways to get through a door. After she'd become a Christian at the beginning of that spring and then led our mom and our brother to the Lord, she'd have her church friends over to the house, supposedly to visit Mom. Her real agenda, though, was to create a setup for them to "talk to Chris about the Lord."

I saw them as being people who just talked…and talked…and talked. As I waited for them to give it a rest, or in other words, shut up, I wondered how people could say so many words in such a short period of time.

Looking back I think that they were nervous because they were talking to the last unsaved person in my family and probably felt some pressure to get me saved. They tried to come off as acting as normal as possible, but in spite of their good intentions, I felt like they were putting on a show for me.

In the midst of all that was going on around me, something my brother did impacted me like nothing else had. He gave me his dope after he got saved. This may sound strange, but when he did that, I knew his faith was real. It was expensive stuff and yet he was giving it away. As he handed it to me, he declared, "I'm not going to need this anymore." I knew that my brother, who was twenty years old at the time, had really been changed. Even though it would seem like the right thing would have been to just throw it out, God used it anyway. My thoughts after he did it were, "Wow, God really did change his life!"

At about the same time, I got a call from my sister asking if I was coming to Brockport for her college graduation ceremony. I said I was. She then asked if I could pick her up at her apartment and give her a ride to the ceremony. My friend Mike had a friend he wanted to visit in the same town so we took off together in his car.

We smoked dope the entire way during the hour-long drive to pick up my sister. The car must have smelled horrible when she and her roommate entered.

I had just moved to the back seat and settled in when my sister, who was now sitting next to me, asked, "Do you remember how I used to always say that some day I'm going to be a princess?"

"Yeah?" I answered cautiously, feeling the full effects of the drugs.

"Well, I am."

"Ah, so you're a princess?" I asked.

"Yep."

"You got married?"

"Yep, I married a prince," she announced.

"And who might that prince be?"

Just as serious as she could be, she said, "Jesus, the Prince of Peace."

My friend Mike looked at me through the rearview mirror and our eyes locked in an exchange that said, "You've got to be kidding!"

Jokingly, I said, "Oh, so you married the Prince of Peace? Was it a nice wedding?"

"Well, it wasn't really a wedding. Now we're married in my heart."

"Oh, wonderful. I sure hope you have a nice life together." I was clearly mocking her.

She then added, "Do you know that I speak in tongues?"

"What?" I asked.

"You remember how in church on Pentecost Sunday we would read something about the Upper Room, and how tongues of fire came down on people and they started speaking in tongues?"

"I think so," I replied.

"Well, I can speak in tongues."

"Okay then, can I hear it?"

"Oh no, it's not like that. I'm not supposed to just say it to you like that."

With each new revelation she shared with us, my friend Mike and I would lock eyes. We could hear each other thinking, "Can you believe this?"

She moved to the next topic, "Have you ever heard of the word *prophecy*?"

"Yeah, it's when people see things that are about to happen," I answered.

"Well, there is that kind of prophecy," she said, "but I mean a simple prophecy of God speaking to someone by sharing encouraging things through somebody else."

"Well, okay, what about it?" I replied.

"Well, I can speak prophetically," she declared.

"You can?" I retorted, no longer even thinly veiling the fact that I thought what she was saying was ridiculous. "So, let me get this straight. God actually speaks through you?"

"Yeah, God speaks through me," she answered matter-of-factly.

Okay. So this is how she witnesses to me. I'm stoned in the back of an Oldsmobile 442, and she tells me that she's married to the Prince of Peace, speaks in tongues, and that God speaks through her.

"So, if God speaks through you, then what does He sound like?" I asked.

She said, "Well, I guess He sounds like me."

At this point I said, "That's horrible. God sounds like you? If God sounds like you, then I don't want anything to do with Him."

To that she said, "He just uses my personality and my voice."

Dying to wrap this up, I stated, "I'm sorry, Carol, but that just doesn't work for me. It's awesome for you."

I had a habit of minimizing her newest interests because I figured they wouldn't last long. She had been up and down with trying new things all the time, and so this seemed like just another addition to a long list of things she'd tried over the years. I figured, "Oh, so now she's doing the Jesus thing." I assumed she'd stick with this about as long as the last thing she'd been into.

Not wanting to waste a moment of the five-minute car ride, she then said, "Have you ever heard of visions, of people having visions?"

"Maybe, kind of, ah...no," I said.

"Our pastor has had visions. God shows him things," she said.

"Well, that's great if God is showing people things, but I don't want your prophecy and I don't want to speak in tongues. If that's good for you and you're happy, then I'm happy for you. Mike and I are happy. Aren't we, Mike?"

Mike nodded and said, "Yep, I'm happy."

"See, Carol, Mike's happy and I'm happy...and we're both happy that you're happy."

Though she did not outwardly show that my mocking comments hurt in any way, she did stop her unusual form of witnessing and began to direct Mike as to where she needed to be dropped off.

As Carol and her friend were getting out of the car, I told her to go ahead without us. We would park the car and be there in a few minutes. When I got into the front seat and shut the door, Mike and I busted out in hysterical laughter. He kept saying he didn't want to laugh too much because it was my sister, but he couldn't hold it back. We both laughed so hard our sides hurt.

My laughter did not last long, however. Mike parked the car and as I was getting out, I heard an audible voice behind me say, "Everything your sister just said is true." Startled, I quickly looked behind me but there was no one there. I looked all around, even glancing into the back seat of the car. Again, there was no one there. I knew, though, that I had heard a voice.

I asked Mike, "Did you hear that?"

He said, "Hear what?"

Then I knew: I was the only one who had heard it.

The instant I shut the car door I completely sobered up. What should have been in my system for another hour or two had instantly disappeared. Mike was still laughing and joking, but because I was now sober, I could only pretend that I thought things were funny. No amount of pretending could take me back to the high we had been sharing just moments earlier. I knew that God had physically touched me and that it was His voice that had spoken clearly and directly to me.

In a five-minute car ride my sister had told me that she had married the Prince of Peace, she was now a princess, she now speaks in tongues, she speaks prophetically, and the leader of her church had visions. No matter how offbeat and silly she had come off, the seed of truth had been planted. At that point I knew that sooner or later it was going to be all over for me. I knew I could fight it for a while, but I knew I wouldn't last. I was alone. I was alone because I was wrong. This, along with my brother giving me his drugs, added up to my feeling absolutely certain that my days of doing things my own way were coming to an end.

My brother thought the old scare tactic might work so he gave me a copy of the book *The Late Great Planet Earth*. He was right. I did get a bit scared after reading a few chapters, so I decided to shelve the end time stuff even though I knew he was really into it. I was in no mood to read about judgments and plagues, and yet part of me knew that there was some truth to this as well. For my brother (always the analytical one), the decision to take his faith to the level of following Jesus as the Lord of his life was based on logic and intellectual deduction. He knew it was the right thing to do.

On the other hand, my sister's journey in going beyond the thin faith we had gained in our small Catholic church was very different from his. She lived in the world of emotion. She was smart—of that there was no doubt—but she had been in the middle of a personal struggle when a college acquaintance started hounding her to turn to Jesus. He had just gotten saved and came off as a real nuisance.

But his relentless presentation of God's plan of salvation, his genuineness, and his sincere love and care for her as a person helped her realize that her life was really a mess and she was a wreck without God's help. God plucked her from the fire when she put her trust in Him.

I knew my time was coming, but I was still putting it off when I heard that my sister was bringing a friend of hers to my cousin's wedding. It was August 18, 1973. I figured Carol and her friend would be double-teaming at the reception to try to convince everybody there to get saved. My avoidance strategy was to sit in a corner and get drunk with my cousin Bob. Carol's friend saw our isolated table as a witnessing opportunity and asked my sister if she thought it would be a good time to share the Lord with me.

By this time my sister must have been pretty frustrated with all of my dodges of her efforts because she discouraged the person from even bothering to try. "I don't think Chris will ever get saved," she said. "He always seems so happy and has great favor, so why in his mind would he see any need for turning to the Lord?"

Of course she did not know the emptiness I felt. I was a good actor. She had no idea that the external accolades I'd received through the years had never been enough to offset how low and small I always felt deep down inside.

When my sister came back home with us after the wedding, my best friend Tom was there at the house. The buzz from the few beers at the reception had totally worn off. We were all having a good time hanging out, watching a little TV, and talking together. I left the room for a few minutes to use the bathroom and then headed to the kitchen to get something to eat. When I came back, Carol was leading Tom in a prayer to receive Jesus.

I stood there stunned and thought, "What is she doing? This is going to change everything!"

In answer to my facial expressions, which progressed from surprise to irritation and finally to disbelief, Tom replied, "This is real, man."

After Tom left, Carol asked me if she could tell me what she had prayed with Tom. I was headed to bed so I told her she could follow me in. Pointing to the bed I said, "Go ahead, have a seat and tell me what happened,"

She began to tell me and then suddenly stopped. "Why don't I pray with you what I prayed with Tom? If we get to a part that you don't want to say or don't believe, just don't say it. Is that okay with you?"

I smiled inwardly and thought to myself, "Boy, is she smooth."

By this time it was one o'clock in the morning and all I wanted to do was to go to bed. I said okay and sat up. We were sitting on opposite ends of my bed. I reached up and pulled the drawstring on the light above us, plunging us into darkness. Breaking the awkward silence I said, "Sorry, I just don't want to do this prayer stuff with the light on. Okay, go ahead."

She led me in a simple, little prayer and I believed every word of it. She'd pray a phrase and I'd repeat what she said. For as long as I could remember, I had believed that Jesus was the Son of God and had died for my sins. I didn't fully know what that meant, but verbalizing my beliefs in that way personalized them for me.

At the end of the short prayer, I said, "Whoa!"

I turned on the light. From head to toe I was covered in goose bumps.

"Cool," she said.

I turned to her and asked, "Do you mind leaving? I'd like to be alone."

"Why?"

"I just need some time alone to contemplate what I just did." I knew she would think that I was going to internalize what had happened and have a little prayer time, but instead, after she walked out the door, I thought, "Good, now I can go to sleep."

I did not know what had just happened to me, but I knew one thing: I did not want to confront God. He'd made me nervous in the parking lot a few months before and I didn't want a repeat performance. And I certainly did not want Him to show up in my room. I had heard stories of God revealing Himself to people, and along with Carol's bizarre testimony, I thought that if I could just get Carol out of the room and quickly turn off the light, the "God stuff" wouldn't happen.

Things went very differently, however. Right after she left the room, I became very conscious of Jesus, of His Presence. He was no longer out there; He was within.

Jesus grabbed my attention throughout the next week by surprising me with answers to the simplest of prayers. For example, if I would pray, "Oh God, if You could just help me," a tractor that had been slowing me down while I was driving my dairy route would, at the exact moment of my prayer, move suddenly to the side of the road so I could pass. Or a bee inside the truck that I hadn't been able to get rid of on my own, after a moment of prayer, would immediately fly out. Or a parking spot in a crowded lot would open up out of the blue the second I prayed. I knew God was not a puppet, but I did realize that He wanted to communicate with me, and me with Him. He was just showing me that He was there. It was now a relationship.

My relationship with Him grew slowly at first. Not yet having been discipled, during this early stage of my new life in Him I still did drugs a couple of times. The first time I got a horrible migraine. The same thing happened the second time. When I was lying in bed sick as a dog, I prayed, "Lord, what's going on? Why do I keep getting these migraines?"

In response to this, a clear thought that I now recognized as being the voice of God responded, "Those drugs are illegal and they're bad for you." Months earlier the Voice of Truth had told me that everything my sister had said was true. And now that same Voice, which I knew was God's, had spoken to me again. This time, though, I was in a personal relationship with the One who had spoken and so I was excited to hear His voice and His answer.

My response was, "Oh yeah, I never thought of that. They're bad for me. So, I guess I shouldn't be doing them, should I?"

Inside I heard a firm yet kind, "No."

"Okay then, I'll stop." And from that moment on I had no more desire for drugs. Having heard Him say that to me made it easy for me to put that former lifestyle behind me.

"Wow, I heard God," I thought. I was amazed, happy, thrilled, and eager to do things His way. Being in an intimate relationship with Him, knowing that He cared for every detail of my life and had my good in mind, made me feel more affirmed than ever.

A few weeks after giving my life to the Lord, I went to one of the Friday night college services held at my sister's church in Brockport. I loved it. People sang their hearts out during worship and the message that night was relevant and even humorous at times. After the service, some friends of Carol's asked if they could pray for me. They said, "You need to be baptized in the Spirit." I said okay and a moment later was surrounded by a group of about ten people touching me or extending their hands toward me. This was all pretty new to me, but I found myself going along with it.

They began to speak in tongues and I could tell that soon they were desperately hoping that I would too. Every now and then they would stop and check on me to see if I could speak in tongues yet. I couldn't and I sure wasn't going to fake anything. Finally after quite a while, they began to give up. The people on the fringes drifted away and soon we all knew that our prayer time was done. The remnant that remained encouraged me to keep pressing in and sooner or later there would be a breakthrough.

I went home that night actually encouraged. I was in no hurry to have some new religious culture that I was not completely sure of be thrust upon me. The early 1970s was a time of not only great spiritual renewal in Jesus, it was also a time of counterfeit spirituality. Many cults were born then and I had no desire to join the ranks.

When I got home, I lay down on my couch and began to read a new book that someone had just given me. It was a balanced presentation of the work of the Holy Spirit. I read a chapter, closed my eyes for just a second, fell deeply asleep and began to dream. In the dream I was walking along a country road. I came to a "T" in the road. Looking right, the road quickly turned into a dirt road and just as quickly it became a wide path that led into brambles and gnarly trees. I knew I was not to go that way. As I looked to the left, I saw a beautiful, white mansion. Suddenly in front of me an old man appeared holding a sign. It said, "Messiah" with an arrow underneath it pointing toward the mansion. I now knew which way to go.

When I reached the mansion, I opened the door and found that there were no rooms. There was just a stairway. I climbed the stairs to the second floor, but again there were no rooms, only more stairs leading to the next floor. I climbed to the next floor and there, on the third floor, the stairs ended. Before me was a round foyer, about twenty feet across. On the opposite side of the foyer were two huge doors, at least fifteen feet high. Standing right in front of the doors was a huge angel.

The angel had its arms folded across its chest and was looking right at me. Somehow I knew that God was on the other side of that door, so I walked up to the angel and asked him to move. He looked down at me and said, "No." With resolve I said, "I need to get in there." With a more serious tone to his voice he said, "You can't go in there. If you do, you will die." I then told him that I didn't care and that I still wanted to go in. He then slowly smiled a very knowing smile and stepped out of the way.

His smile actually made me a little nervous, but I didn't care. I was going in. I walked up to the door and grabbed the handle. It was huge. I pulled but the door didn't budge. The angel was still smiling. I gave him a quick, fake-polite smile back and grabbed the handle once more. This time I used both hands and pulled with all my might. The door began to move, but ever so slowly. It was a very thick door, and as I pulled it back, I could see its thickness. I had pulled it at least half a foot when finally the inside edge of the door was visible.

Suddenly, through the crack between the doors, a shaft of intense light from top to bottom came streaking through. It was not just visible, it was physical. It hit me and knocked me back across the foyer. I slammed into the opposite wall and slowly sunk to the ground. A moment later the light around me began to fade and everything went black. I found myself back in my house, fully awake, and speaking in tongues.

I was speaking in tongues! I couldn't believe it. Then I remembered something I had just read earlier that night—that He is the one Who baptizes. Now I knew it for myself.

I was now fully on board with this new life in God. I loved it. I loved His Word, I loved worshipping with other believers, and I loved the joy that came from relationships based on life instead of drugs. I knew it was about Jesus, but something unusual would soon happen in a very dramatic way that would change my life forever.

CHAPTER 6

Face to Face

Standing there, I realized that we were not looking at each other, but instead, our gaze was straight ahead at his garden. It was a beautiful garden, but oh, how I longed to be able to look directly into his eyes. Maybe someday, maybe soon. Let it be, Lord.

———

SOON AFTER BEING FILLED WITH THE SPIRIT, I had another encounter with the Lord that seemed so radical that I kept it to myself for a very long time. I had moved to where my sister and my brother were now both living, Brockport, New York. We were all attending a small but vibrant church that had great teaching and made worship a priority. Saying it was a college town would be an understatement. The town's population actually doubled from 11,000 to 22,000 when school was in session.

Young people were getting saved left and right, not just in Brockport, but also all across the USA. The era would later be referred to in church history as the "Jesus Movement." We were at the tail end of it. In Brockport, every Friday night, hundreds of young people packed in like sardines into a building that was supposed to hold maybe 150 to 200 people. During those times you could barely breathe, yet so many kids would come. Hundreds of lives were being changed forever.

I was no longer working at the dairy, which was now an hour's drive from Brockport. Instead, I worked at a local hospital ordering and distributing supplies within the hospital. I often went back to my little second-floor apartment for lunch. The people living downstairs worked the night shift. They too were believers and their home group met in their apartment at noon one day a week. On the days they met, I would run home, stand over the ventilation grate in my living room, and listen to the beautiful worship music below me as I ate my typical lunch, which was a bologna sandwich with mayonnaise on white bread. I didn't have my wonderful wife Laura yet.

One particular afternoon I was standing above the grate with my eyes closed, enjoying the music and my sandwich. I suddenly felt a breeze blowing on me. When I opened my eyes to see if I had left a door or a window open, I certainly never expected to see what I saw. Instead of seeing the familiar setting of my apartment, I was jolted by the realization that I was literally standing in the open air on a hillside. My sandwich was gone, but I had on the same clothes.

I quickly took stock of the situation: I did not lay down on my bed to go to sleep, I was not on drugs, and I was not hallucinating. I was actually standing on a hillside.

Baffled, I asked myself, "What in the world is going on?"

The hillside I was on was in a park. Scattered throughout the park were groups of people picnicking together. Hamburgers were grilling. Kids were playing. Dogs were running around and barking. The scene was very inviting.

I then noticed several people walking by me who were headed up the hill that sloped upwards behind me. Somehow I knew they were

An early official Air Force picture showing my father's bright blue eyes. So young and without a clue as to what will happen soon.

My mother was not only a pilot, she taught others to fly until an insecure male officer said it was not good for moral to have a woman teaching men to fly. He "promoted" her to an office secretarial position.

My mother after her "promotion."

My mother was so carefree when she was young. She loved the freedom that came with riding horses.

My mother was a beautiful woman, inside and out.

My father (in the middle) surrounded by his sister Jane and his three brothers. As the sign reads on the wagon, the year was 1931.

My father and his brother Pete, before the fighting.

From crutches to a cane. Soon Dad will be walking. Other wounds will take a bit longer to heal.

My father is reunited with his brother, Pete, after returning from Germany.

There's my mom, carefree and ready to serve.

A hero with his medals.

With my parents shortly after I was born.
The look on my mother's face says it all.

One of my dad's favorite places—the classroom. He was the consummate teacher.

My father and his brothers at their favorite place—the St. Lawrence River. Thumbs up, Dad!

Department of Veterans Affairs

POSTHUMOUS

Commendation

This certificate is awarded to

The Family of David J. DuPré

David DuPré was a WWII ex-POW who was an inspiration to all who knew him. A man of warmth, honesty and integrity, he was a staunch advocate for all veterans, especially for those who would not or could not stand up for themselves. Always concerned with veterans' services, he was a strong and loyal supporter of us all in the Department of Veterans Affairs when we needed and deserved it, an outspoken but fair voice of criticism if he felt we were not doing our jobs properly. That combination of empathy, dedication and candor is what made him such a special and irreplaceable friend to us all.

Given at   VA Outpatient Clinic
Rochester, NY

This 20th *day of*   September   19 91.

WILLIAM H. MANLEY
Medical Center Director

A posthumous award given to my father to honor him for all the work he did with veterans over the years. It speaks to his empathy, dedication, and candor. He was an inspiration to so many.

We won the sectionals that day. It was my senior year. I'm on the left with the muscular legs. Ah, those were the days.

Thursday, November 12, 1970 B2

MARION BOOTERS—Comprising the Marion Central School ... ty soccer team are (front from left) Steve Dulmage, ... Huber, Bruce Stone, Tom Haak, Gordon DePoint (co- Terry Krocke, Paul De Point, Mike Erb; (back from left) Coach Chuck Bailey, Jim Adriaansen, Karl Bueg, Tom Spittal, Chris DuPre, Howard Bush (co-capt.), Dave Sewert, John Kymble, Jay McLouth, Rafael Mella, Jim Thomas. Absent is Gary Scrooby.

I'm in the center of the second row standing next to my best friend, Tom, on my right. We were saved on the same day almost three years later.

Four ribbons from one week in track. I had to show I won something.

My grandmother's home was a place of safety and peace for me. An amazing woman!

My grandmother in her late 80s. She lived 99 meaningful years.

Wow, we're really married, and yes, I did marry up!

My lovely, little girls when they were young with me and my Tom Selleck mustache.

The love of my life. She is the essence of true beauty.

My beautiful girls. I'm a blessed man.

With my wife, Laura, at our favorite place, Coast Guard Beach on
Cape Cod.

believers. As they passed me, they said, "You might as well come because they're not listening anymore. All they want to do is eat and drink and have fun."

It was evident to me that they had just finished speaking with all of the people who were at the picnic, but none of the people wanted to hear any more of what they had to say.

The followers of Jesus then said to me, "By the way, He's coming."

While I was walking up the hill with the other believers, I was wondering, "What am I doing outside walking up a hill when I'm supposed to be in my apartment eating my lunch?"

To test the reality of the situation, I reached down, plucked a piece of grass, and ate it. It was real all right. It tasted just like grass. I spit it out. Next, I pinched myself. Sure enough, it hurt. These two quick reality checks convinced me that something about all of this was real.

The hill we were walking up was not large. When I reached the top, I joined a circle of about thirty other people. They said to me, "You know He's coming soon." As we stood together and waited, I wondered if Jesus was really coming.

After a few minutes I noticed everyone around me was looking up. I looked up and saw why. As if being lowered on a cable, Jesus was coming down right into the center of the circle. He had on a long robe and was barefoot. I could not see His face as He was facing the opposite direction. Long dark hair poured over the back of His robe.

I then thought of those poor people at the bottom of the hill who were having fun but were missing out on all of this.

My eyes were wide as I kept them fixed on Him and took note of His every movement. I could tell that He was now looking at those in front of Him. He gazed at each of them, one at a time.

"Before long it will be my turn," I thought.

"Soon, He will be looking at me."

"Hey, wait. He'll see everything. I don't want Him to see everything."

I felt an urge to run as I thought, "This is not what I signed up for!"

"But, I don't want to run."

Finally, His face came into view. I could see the left side of His cheek.

I thought, "Oh no, He's angry!"

His face looked tense and his cheeks were scrunched up.

Then, suddenly, to my surprise, when He came around and I could see more of the front of his face, I realized his expression wasn't anger at all.

Instead, it was the largest smile I had ever seen!

He went from person to person and suddenly, He set His gaze upon me. No one had ever looked at me like that! He was looking right through me and filling every pore and every crevice of my being with light and love. The words, "Wild Love" filled my mind and heart. Wild Love! Because of His wild love, He was not constrained by anything or anyone. Nothing or no one had the power or the ability to hinder Him from loving me, deeply and fully.

I could still feel His love for me when He moved around the circle of people and looked at each of the others in the same way. When He was done, He got down on one knee, stretched His hand toward us, and said, "It's time to go, My Beloved. Come away with Me."

Three years later, He would explain to me why He had bent down on one knee. I was telling someone the story of when I had asked Laura to marry me, and as I was recounting that precious moment, the Lord said to me, "Remember, I got down on one knee for you, too." Knowingly and thankfully, I would respond in my thoughts and from my heart, "Yes, Lord, I remember. You did do that for me, didn't You."

Standing from His bended knee, Jesus told us that it was time to go. He began to rise in the air. A number of people in the group also began to ascend, but I was still just standing there. I was beginning to feel very heavy. I felt like I weighed a thousand pounds. People all around me were rising, but I was firmly planted on the ground. Just before I cried out to Him for help, I too began to rise. I couldn't believe it. I was lifting off the ground! I pinched myself again and like the first time, it hurt. As we continued to rise, the air around us became cooler, the wind began to pick up, and the world became a more distant place.

We rose until we were five miles above the earth. I don't know how, but I knew it was five miles. I just knew. There was a platform right in the middle of the air and He placed us all there. He said He had to return to earth and take care of some things, but that He would return to us soon. We all settled back to wait. I sat on the side of the platform and dangled my feet over the edge. As I was looking down, I wondered what Jesus was doing down there. I noticed that after a few minutes someone sat down next to me. I glanced over and realized that it was Jesus. I could see His feet and His clothes out of the corner of my eye.

I assumed that if this really was the end times, Jesus would not be next to me; He would be next to each person. I turned around to see if He was standing next to everyone else. Much to my surprise, He was not. As a matter of fact, they were all looking at me, and for some reason I could hear their thoughts. In unison they were asking, "Why is He with you?" With palms up, I lifted my hands to the side, shrugged my shoulders, and with a questioning look I silently mouthed out the words, "I don't know."

I turned around to talk to Jesus but I froze. What do I say to the Son of God? I mean, seriously; He knows everything. He created me. I suddenly thought of talking to Him about the book of Deuteronomy. I figured that would make me look like a serious and well-read Christian. I didn't really know anything about Deuteronomy, but I hoped that He would be impressed and that He would carry the conversation from there.

I began to lift my head, but I could not look into His face. I saw the hair on the back of His hands and His long flowing dark hair, but I could not look directly into His eyes. I knew if I did, He would see right through me, right into my soul, right into my sin. I lifted my head enough to see His beard. It was not a well-trimmed beard like most men have today. Instead I could see little hairs that grew down toward the neck. I could tell that He was looking at me; I just couldn't look at Him. I again tried to lift my head but I couldn't. Instead, I said, "Lord, I, I..." and then I quickly dropped my head in shame. I then whispered, "I'm sorry." I felt like a fake. I was sure I didn't love Him as much as the other people standing behind me did, and I was also sure that at any moment, Jesus was going to expose my hypocritical heart in front of all the others.

Suddenly I felt His strong hands on both sides of my face. He lifted my head and looked right into my eyes. We were less than a foot apart. I tried to drop my head again but He took His right hand and put it under my chin, forcing me to look directly at Him. I finally lifted my eyes and looked directly into His. Wild love struck me once again. His look told me that no one controlled how deeply and how passionately He loved. His dark brown eyes were filled with warmth and affection. No face had ever looked so full of grace and love. I was undone.

He looked deeply into my eyes, smiled, and gently said, "Shhh." He then said, "I love you. You need to know that. For what I have planned for you, you will need to know that." He then took my head and laid it upon His breast. He put His arms around me and held me close. He then started to rock me like a father would rock his own child. Suddenly I began to cry, gently at first, but within a short period of time, I began to weep from deep within my soul. I realized at that moment that my own father had never held me like this.

Now I had Jesus' arms around me, holding me tight. I felt safe and at home. As I continued to cry, He leaned over and with a soft voice began to whisper in my ear, "I love you. It's all right. I'm here. You need to know how deeply I love you." He filled me with comfort, continued to rock me, and then He lovingly kissed my head. Suddenly a ball of fire shot from out of His heart and into mine. It hit me like I'd been punched in the chest with a sledgehammer. I fell backward and found myself back in my apartment.

I saw my bed, went over, and lay down. I was still crying deep heavy sobs that wouldn't stop. After a while, I finally came to the end of my tears. I began to sit up and noticed how wet my pillow was. I lifted my pillow and saw that it was dripping from the bottom. I had wept through my pillow! I put my hand on the area of my mattress that had been directly under my pillow and as I pushed down, water bubbles came up between my fingers. I had not only wept through my pillow, I had even soaked my mattress with my tears. How long had I been crying and what had brought on all those tears?

A few days later, someone asked me a question about my father. Usually when something about my father would come up, I would instantly feel an ache in the pit of my stomach. This time, though, I felt nothing negative. As a matter of fact, I felt great warmth toward my dad, even compassion. I felt no hurt or pain. I tried. I thought of events that had produced pain in the past, but there was nothing in me that hurt. Instead, I began to feel a deep understanding and compassion for what he must have gone through while he was a prisoner of war.

I then knew what had happened to me that day. Jesus had hugged me and rocked the pain right out of me as His wild love washed over me and through me. Tears of healing had flowed from me and I now felt like a different person.

Knowing the Father's Heart

So, how was I supposed to begin? Though I could clearly hear my father talking about this year's crop, all that was going through my mind was, "What do I say? Better yet, what will he say? Maybe this isn't a good idea. Yeah, there's probably a better time to do this than at a Fourth of July party with all the family around. What was I thinking?" Then I realized…it wasn't my thinking that had me here. It was His, my Father's, and one thing I knew: He had only good for me. All right, Papa, I trust You.

———

I DIDN'T KNOW OF ANYONE who'd had an experience like the one I'd had. Carol had mentioned that her pastor had had a vision, but when I heard him describe it, it was nothing like what I had just gone through. I decided not to tell anybody about what had just happened to me. I felt like the best way to protect the work God had done in me (and was still doing) was to not open myself up to the slightest possibility of someone convincing me that maybe I had just been exhausted and had taken a nap, or had eaten a bad piece of bologna, or the tears were actually water that had spilled on my pillow.

People did notice a change in me and a few even vocalized their thoughts, asking me what was different. My brother took me by surprise shortly after when he said, "You're still funny, but there's something more of a man about you. I don't know what's going on with you, but there's a settledness in you that didn't used to be there."

I told him, "I think I know what happened. I had a little face-to-face with Jesus recently."

"That must have been it," he said. "Now you don't always turn everything into a joke. I mean, I always knew there was depth in you, I just hadn't seen it much." I smiled at his backhanded compliment. I love my brother.

Looking back, I now know I had been using humor to cover up what was really going on inside of me, but experiencing Jesus' wild love for me had melted away my insecurities and built my confidence up to a level where I was able to start showing people the real me. I was also looking forward to seeing who the real me was.

A bullet was shot into my fearful heart when I saw and experienced Jesus' wild love. I understood that Jesus' love for me and the Father's love for me were the same love. Up until that time, it had been hard for me to read Scriptures about God the Father. Jesus had always fascinated me and the Holy Spirit had always seemed pretty mysterious (as a Catholic, the Holy Spirit was always referred to as the Holy Ghost), but I'd always assumed that the Father wasn't crazy about me. I knew He loved me. I just thought, because He was God, He had to.

Like most people, my view of God the Father had been shaped by my relationship with my natural father and other authority figures in my life. Experiencing Jesus' wild love for me changed my opinion of what God thought about me and, in turn, changed what I thought about myself, what I thought about God, and what I thought about others. I learned firsthand that our view of the Father will always be faulty if it is based on our success or failure in human relationships. Our view of the Father also will cloud our view of others and ourselves. Because I had thought the Father was judgmental, I thought I was always being judged in a negative way. This had led to my being judgmental of others and of myself.

I was so blinded by my assumption that I didn't measure up to God's demands that I hadn't been able to see the love of God right in front of me in His Word. Up until that time, I had skimmed over Scriptures like:

> I pray that you, being rooted and established in love, may have power, together with all the saints, to grasp how wide and long and high and deep is the love of Christ, and to know this love that surpasses knowledge—that you may be filled to the measure of all the fullness of God (Ephesians 3:18-19 NIV).

Now I was thrilled and elated at the prospect of a life of discovering how much God loves me and of being "filled to the measure of all the fullness of God."

Everywhere I turned in Scripture, in the Old Testament as well as in the New, I saw the ways in which He loved me. Where I had only seen judgment in the past, I now saw His love.

When Jesus was looking at someone in the Word, I was the one He was looking at. In the past, His face was a blank to me. Now that I had looked deeply into his bright eyes and had been comforted by the tenderness of His smile, I was right there in the middle of all of the accounts of what He was doing. It may have happened 2000 years ago, but it was as though I was right there. In an instant, His gaze into my eyes forever changed the way I gaze into His.

So what does that? How does all of that happen in an instant? I am convinced that the heart is moved when the eyes behold. It's in the beholding, the place where we really see, that our heart can be moved upon by Him. We all notice things, but not all of us behold. We do it with people and we do it with God.

That was the case the day I met my wife, Laura. It was early in the spring of 1977. I had moved to Schenectady, New York, earlier in the year and was now being invited to play softball with some friends. When I arrived at the game, I noticed a girl talking to a man who was later identified as the pastor of a nearby church. She had dark hair that flowed past her waist and she wore a poncho that almost completely covered her. She spent the afternoon engrossed in conversation, her thoughts definitely not on the game.

After the game a group decided to go to a local pizza place. I was to ride with a friend but found myself in a conversation after the game and missed my ride. I assumed the person I was talking with was also going out for pizza, but it turned out that instead, he needed to go home. I headed to the parking lot, hoping that someone was still there with a car and would want to join the others for pizza.

Upon arriving, poncho girl saw me and asked me if I could help her start her car. Her father had helped her purchase the car earlier that very day. It was a tiny 1977 Honda Civic with a standard transmission and a manual choke. She was not comfortable with the car yet, especially the manual choke, which she didn't even know existed.

I came over and showed her what the choke was and how it worked, started up the car, and asked her if she was going for pizza. She said yes and I volunteered to drive us over. We joined our group of friends and ended up having a very pleasant evening. After that, I saw her fairly regularly as I ended up going to the church she attended, and she would come to a coffeehouse our group held on Friday and Saturday nights.

There was nothing romantic going on between us, just a nice friendship surrounded by a group of mutual friends. As time went by, my roommate, who had been spending quite a bit of time with her, mentioned that Laura might be interested in me. I laughed it off and said that since he spent so much time with her, why didn't he just start going out with her. He said she was not interested in him.

I liked her as a friend, but was not interested in her in any other way. She was an amazing person who (and I really did say this) would one day make someone a wonderful wife. I even said she's the kind of girl I'd want to marry someday. Not her specifically, just that kind of girl, whatever that meant. As time passed, I was busy with life and I heard she had taken a job nearby. I didn't see her as often, but my friend still made sure to carve out time to hang with her.

A couple of months later I was at a friend's house for a party. It was an open house kind-of-thing and people were arriving and departing all evening long. I was across the room from the front door when this beautiful girl with dark, shoulder-length hair walked in. She was stunning.

I turned to my friend and asked, "Who is that girl?"

"That's Laura," he said.

I asked him, "Laura who?"

That's when he looked at me like I had just arrived from outer space. With a bit of an attitude he said, "That's Laura Rocissano."

I looked at her as if it were the first time. I said, "She's beautiful."

He turned to me, looked me right in the eyes and said, "Well, it's about time you saw what everyone else has always known. Yes, Laura is beautiful and for some strange reason, I think she likes you." Ten months later we were married.

I found out later that on the first day we met, she had stood in the parking lot next to her car waiting for everyone else to pass by before she asked me to help her with her car. I've always liked that part of the story best.

So why is it that we can know the same person, see the same face, and yet not see the real beauty that is there. Two people can look at the same person and they can each see something very different. I did it. I saw Laura at least once a week for months but I never saw her true beauty until one fine day when my eyes were opened. That's the key—eyes that don't just look at something or someone, but eyes that really see the beauty that is there.

Paul addresses this in his letter to the Ephesians. Ephesus, foremost of the Asian churches, was rich beyond measure in Jesus, yet they were beggars in their hearts. They were surrounded by the grace of God and yet they could not see it. He describes in the first few chapters all that they possess in Him—from adoption, forgiveness, redemption, inheritance, grace, and so much more; and yet, before he goes on, he prays for them. They need God's help in order to truly see God.

In Ephesians 1:16-18, he turns his message into a prayer. He says, I... "do not cease to give thanks for you, making mention of you in my prayers. That the God of our Lord Jesus Christ, the Father of Glory, may give to you the spirit of wisdom and revelation in the knowledge of Him, the eyes of your understanding being enlightened."

Paul was praying, not for more wisdom or revelation, though in itself more of each would be a good thing. He was asking the Lord to give them wisdom as to who He is and revelation of His true nature.

Paul was saying that wisdom and revelation are first and foremost given to the church to see Jesus in His fullness. To see Him for Who He is. He realized that we have eyes that see what's before us, but that each of us is given another set of eyes, the eyes of our understanding. You can see that it takes a revelation *from* God to have a revelation *of* God.

I finally understood what the eyes of my understanding were when I saw Laura that one night. I had seen her, but I had never really seen her. Everyone around me kept singing her praises, but for some reason, the eyes of my understanding were blinded. In one day, though, it all changed. From the moment I truly *saw* her, I was then able to begin to fully *love* her.

So too, with God, just a glance of the real Him can change everything. That's why Paul prayed for the Ephesians. He understood that if God answers our prayers to see Him more clearly, we will love Him more deeply. The two go hand in hand, with people and with God.

In chapter 3 Paul goes even further. In verse 14 he "bows his knee," in prayer again, asking that God would grant them "to be strengthened with might through His spirit in the inner man." There it is again. This inner man with inner eyes, the eyes of understanding, needs God's help to see the beauty that is always right there in front of us.

The importance of seeing clearly was further brought home to me one day when I met a gentleman at a church function. Those introducing him had told me what an incredible man he was and they were excited that we were finally meeting. He seemed nice, but also detached, and he also seemed to be in a hurry to go somewhere. I must admit I was not extremely impressed with the man. A short time later I met a young man at a pick-up basketball game. He was fun to be with as well as a great player. We had a wonderful time and ended up going out for a bite to eat after the game. In the midst of our conversation, it became apparent that he was the son of the man I had met earlier at the church function.

What changed in me was that in the son, I saw someone of incredible life. He radiated joy and had a depth about him way beyond his years. This, of course, did not come out of a vacuum. I saw in his eyes and heard in his voice the well that was his father. When I asked about his dad, he talked on and on with such love and reverence that I was overwhelmed. He also made mention of some distressing news that his dad had just heard and that was weighing on him deeply at the time I had met him.

It all made sense. I learned a couple of lessons that day. One was the ongoing lesson not to judge others so quickly, but an even greater lesson and revelation came my way. I was able to see the father through the son. A light that had been switched on soon after my face-to-face experience with Jesus became even brighter. I need the Son to be able to know. I need the Son to be able to see. I need to know and see the Son, here and now, so that I can more fully see the Father's smile and understand the affection He has for me.

Experiencing Jesus' wild love for me was the doorway for me to see, know, and experience the love of the Father. Whether I was spending intimate time with Him in reading the Bible, praying, or just living out my daily life, at every turn the Holy Spirit was unveiling Jesus, and therein unveiling the Father to me. Jesus said:

> "If you had known Me, you would have known My Father also; from now on you know Him, and have seen Him." Philip said to Him, "Lord, show us the Father, and it is enough for us." Jesus said to him, "Have I been so long with you, and yet you have not come to know Me, Philip? He who has seen Me has seen the Father; how can you say, 'Show us the Father'? Do you not believe that I am in the Father, and the Father is in Me? The words that I say to you I do not speak on My own initiative, but the Father abiding in Me does His works. Believe Me that I am in the Father and the Father is in Me; otherwise believe because of the works themselves" (John 14:7-11 NASB).

"If you had known me, you would have known my Father." What a stunning statement. If we see Jesus, we see the Father. Said differently, whatever we see of Jesus is what we see of the Father. Whatever we understand about Jesus, we understand about the Father. This was a huge revelation for me. To transfer understanding or knowledge from Jesus to the Father had not been easy for me. I easily got that they both are all-knowing, all-powerful, and eternal. But to trust that this Father has the same heart, love, and emotions as Jesus required an extension of my own emotions that was far beyond my comfort zone. I had always seen Jesus as the understanding One. He was full of grace and mercy for even the most vile of sinners. He knew pain and was acquainted with sorrow and grief. But the Father, well, He was distant. He probably just put up with me for Jesus' sake.

Through those words and similar passages, Jesus extends an invitation to all of us. It's as if He is saying, "Hey, here I am. Do you see Me? If you do, look carefully. Gaze upon Me and you will see My Father. I love because He loves; I heal because He heals, and I speak because He speaks. When you glimpse an aspect of My essence, you are glimpsing Father God as well. Jesus also said:

> "The Son can do nothing of Himself, unless it is something He sees the Father doing; for whatever the Father does, these things the Son also does in like manner" (John 5:19a NASB).

> "The word which you hear is not Mine, but the Father's who sent Me" (John 14:24b NASB).

When I read Jesus' words, "He who has seen Me has seen the Father," I knew that they implied, "When you see me expressing my love, you see the Father expressing His love." In light of my own experience, this meant that Jesus' expressions of His wild love for me were expressions of the Father's wild love for me. But being able to see the Father in this way would require the help of the Holy Spirit. Thankfully, Jesus promised:

> "But the Helper, the Holy Spirit, whom the Father will send in My name, He will teach you all things, and bring to your remembrance all things that I said to you" (John 14:26).

My face-to-face time with Jesus had ignited my yearning to know and experience even more of the width, length, height, and depth of His love for me. Because Jesus is the Door, the Window, the Gate, and every other entry point into every dimension or aspect of the Father, my growing relationship with Him brought me face to face with multi-faceted layers of my false view of the Father that had also clouded my view of myself and other people.

Hebrews says that Jesus is "the radiance of God's glory and the exact representation of His being." It's pretty clear that He is "the exact representation." He has the exact look, the exact heart, thoughts, desires, capacity to love, everything. Everything that Jesus is, the Father is. Therefore, when you look at Jesus, you're looking at the Father. It doesn't get more simple or more beautiful than that.

The Journey of Forgiveness

Okay, so how long do I stand here? My dad is talking and pointing at one plant after another and I'm right beside him, appearing connected; yet my mind is wandering all over the universe. One minute I'm going back over my past, the next minute I'm crafting words for my immediate future.

Come on, Chris, you can do this. Remember, you're not alone.

ABOUT A YEAR PREVIOUSLY, during our time living in New York City, I had met a gentleman who had gone through a very similar situation with his own father. His dad had been very abusive for many years, and yet as he talked about him, I could hear the love in his heart for his father. I was amazed that what had once been a cold and indifferent relationship had grown over time into a loving and caring father-son bond. It was a simple yet compelling story of love and forgiveness, and its impact penetrated deeply into my soul.

He spoke of giving the "the gift of forgiveness" to his dad every time he saw him. Finally, after many years, his father slowly began to express love back to him, in small ways at first, but over time those small ways grew in size and number. God used that message to encourage me that things with my dad could, and hopefully would, one day be resolved. But He also made it clear that at some point, I would need to be the one to do the initial reaching out. God wanted me to pursue my father.

The perfect follow-up scenario would have me jumping into my car that very day and get it all resolved right then and there. But I knew better. Trying to pattern my journey after another's could have damaging results. Only God knew when I would be ready to put the gift of my forgiveness on the altar and leave it there without any expectations.

In my own secret desires, though, prying open that door on my own would have looked something like this: I would share with my dad all the horrible things he had done; my dad would cry crocodile tears and repent (loudly and humbly); he would then readily admit his own guilt (in great detail); and finally, he would vow before heaven and earth that he would never, ever hurt me again. It all reminded me of an old song, "The Impossible Dream." As I said, I knew better.

After our year in New York City, moving back to Rochester in 1981 was a concrete step toward my dad. I had been carrying within me the knowledge that God wanted me to make a greater heart connection with him. Being in the same city where he lived would make spending time with him on a regular basis more possible. What actually happened when we did get together, well, that was another question.

It was planting season on a number of levels when Dad began having us over for lunch or dinner periodically after Laura and I moved back to Rochester. It was March of 1981, just as spring was arriving. At that time we had just one child, our daughter Andrea. That spring, summer, or fall, if we came for lunch, Dad was usually in the middle of gardening or watching a TV program about gardening. Each visit was a mini-tour to show me what he'd planted that week and how all the other vegetables he'd planted earlier in the season were doing.

Each time he offered these new seeds into our relationship, I accepted them wholeheartedly by being very purposeful to show him that I was interested in what was clearly very important to him. He often started our times together in the garage. He would show me some seed packets or what was to soon be planted. I asked him a lot of questions and gave him positive feedback to let him know that I valued the work he was doing and appreciated his sharing this part of his life with me. His updates and my interest always led up to the two of us strolling out back so he could show me the garden's progress. These moments would then take a slow turn toward my sowing seeds into our relationship as well when I would tell him about some of the events of my life and nudge him and Marian a little closer to my new family with Laura.

From the start, my dad had been very happy in his second marriage. Though he always tried to have a garden wherever we had lived, after his second marriage, gardening took on a new level of joy and pride. These two areas—his marriage and his gardens—seemed to indicate that he was settling into a new level of peace. Looking back, I'd have to say that it was like the ground of his life was being leveled out much in the same way that you dig up the fallow ground, add a bit more dirt, and smooth it out before planting. God had been taking debris, rocks, stones, and dead things out of the ground of his heart while he was getting counseling and just living life. I could see that having someone to love and also being loved was bringing a new softness and settledness to him.

Because of his tireless work with veterans, our local congressman made Dad the top Veteran's Affairs advocate in the district. I should have been celebrating all these new successes with him. Instead, my attention had been on Marian's kids telling me from time to time, "Wow, your dad sure is harsh." There it was. The man so beloved on the outside was still struggling at home. Because a lot of debris was still blocking my ability to see the work that God was doing in my dad's life, I remained focused on what tidbits came my way that seemed to confirm my own negative experiences with him.

I should have been cheering for him. I was trying to in the areas of his garden and in his new marriage, but I could not fully see him without seeing a cruel man somewhere in the background just waiting to emerge. I was beginning to celebrate where he was, but who he had been and who he was becoming, that was still being worked out.

As far as my connection with my dad, the year between 1981 and 1982 was a mixed bag. On one hand, I knew in my heart that there would be some form of reconciliation between us. On the other, in spite of my encounter with Jesus and experiencing His love face to face, I still found myself trapped behind a wall of intimidation. I had compassion for him and in my heart there was desire to see things change, but when push came to shove, I kept reverting back to the little kid who was more afraid of him than was confident in love. It would take one more step for me.

During April of 1982, my daughter, Katie, was born. She was a pistol right from the start, very independent and never afraid to express what she was thinking. Even as a newborn, Laura and I could see we had a strong and fearless little girl. As we brought her home and tended to her as parents, something new struck my heart.

Though we already had one child, our daughter Andrea, suddenly having two children made my role as a father different. With one child, a father's role can be limited. But with two, there's always a need to be engaged as a father. That got me thinking.

Now that we, his kids, were older, did our father ever feel loss for the years of separation? I guess I never thought about it. I just assumed that he liked things the way they were. Then I thought, he had three kids and I knew that although he was working through his own hell, he was home and he was somewhat engaged with our lives, no matter how warped it might have been.

If that was true, he must feel loss for the empty years. I know he had great love for his new wife, Marian, and that he and his brothers were inseparable. If he could love them, he must have loved us. He just didn't know how to express it in the midst of his pain. Home had been his prison. He had been responsible for everything, and yet everything seeped through his hands like water. But now that we were grown, now that we were no longer his responsibility, could he now embrace us like he'd always wanted but never could?

That was the question that needed to be answered, and the only way to answer it was to step up to the plate and swing. The plate was the edge of the garden and all I had to swing was the gift of forgiveness.

"The gift of forgiveness." What a wonderful concept. Forgiveness is a lifelong lesson for many. I know it has been for me. Thinking back to when I was twelve, my dad brought my brother, Mark, and me to Canada to attend *Man and His World*, the 1967 World's Fair held in Montreal. It was one of the many times we ventured into Canada with my father while on our yearly, two-week vacation with him. We stayed with relatives in a nice, downtown apartment and left early in the morning to have a full day at the fair.

Walking through the lobby, we saw a man doing tile work. My father said to him, "Good day," and passed by. Wanting to say the right thing, I also said, "Good day," and like my father, smiled and walked by. When we got out onto the busy sidewalk, my father turned around, and in front of a very crowded Montreal street, slapped me hard across the face. It was so hard that I started to fall backwards, but my brother caught me.

People stopped to stare, then slowly began to walk on. I was stunned. I looked at him and saw that he was fuming. I held my hand to my face and said, "What was that for?" He said, "Because of your sarcastic and mocking comment to that man back there." I had no idea what he meant. He turned and started to walk away.

My brother stood next to me and said, "Are you okay?" I wanted to cry, but I wouldn't give my father the satisfaction. Then my brother said, "I think Dad felt you were mocking him and the man working back there by repeating exactly what he had said." I told him I wasn't trying to mock anyone when we heard our father say, "Come on boys, we don't have all day." Actually we did. All week too, but at that moment, I didn't want to spend even the next minute with him.

I was mad and I was going to hold onto my anger as long as I could. It would be my "special gift" to my dad. The gift of "unforgiveness."

We left and headed to the fair *Man and His World*. My father acted as if nothing had happened, which only made things worse. We parked and joined the throng of happy people. I was part of the throng, but not the happy.

Like a child who runs away from home only to return later in the day when he's hungry (I actually did that when I was five), being at a World's Fair when you're angry is a very hard thing to do, especially when you're twelve. There were games, rides, attractions, and every kind of junk food imaginable. I was in heaven. The only problem was, I couldn't let my dad know that I was having a good time. I had to cloak it with a sullen and angry face. Oh, I was still angry, I just couldn't enjoy my anger as much as I would have liked.

After a couple of hours, my father leaned over to me and said, "Mark told me you weren't trying to be mocking. I'm sorry I hit you." I couldn't look him in the eye, so I just nodded and grunted, "Okay." It took a while to let go, but eventually I found myself smiling and enjoying the day. I realized that my dad was trying, which strangely gave me a bit of compassion, allowing myself to let go of my anger and forgive him in my heart, at least as much as I knew how. After that, the slapping event was largely forgotten and mostly forgiven. Total forgiveness would come later.

Another lesson in forgiveness happened the summer before my senior year of high school. I saw a girl at our county fair (uh-oh, sounds like trouble already). She had been going out with a guy I had only just met, but she told me that they had recently broken up.

We had a conversation and then spent the evening walking around the fair taking in the sights. We had a nice time. It was all very innocent and we never saw each other after that night. A couple of weeks later, her old boyfriend gathered four other guys and jumped me from behind in a parking lot. Five on one was not a fair fight, and I ended up bruised, bloodied, and unconscious. A friend pulled me into a car and drove me home.

The result of that fight was that in my heart, I was now battling a combination of hatred and fear. This guy lived in another town, so I never knew where he was. Because of sports, I had to travel to other towns constantly, so I was always looking over my shoulder for any kind of suspicious movement. I had no desire to forgive the guy. It wasn't even in my thoughts. I felt too empowered by anger and hatred.

It turned out that he wasn't done with me. It was now March of my senior year. That old boyfriend of hers was once again her new boyfriend and he couldn't bear the thought that someone else had his girlfriend's heart, even for a night. After a night of heavy drinking, he pulled together three carloads of guys and headed for my house.

My best friend, Tom, heard about it and called to warn me. Good thing, because I was on my way to answer a knock at the door when he called. The first thing he said was, "If someone knocks on your door, do not answer it." I reached over and locked the door. They knocked again, but I ignored it. Tom told me that they had been to his house and were looking for me. His father chased them away with a shotgun.

I wondered how they knew where I lived until Tom said that a kid from our class was with them, and he said he would guide them to my house. Well, he sure did. I looked out the side window of my home and saw three cars parked down the street. In the hands of one guy I saw a tire iron, and in another's hands were some chains. I felt like I was in a bad movie.

I didn't feel safe in my own house, so I jumped out a back window and headed to my cousin's house across town. I called the cops who quickly came and sent the cars home. They followed up with a restraining order against each of the guys from the other town. The one that slipped through the cracks was the kid from my class. I would deal with him myself.

The following week I found the kid at his locker. He turned around and there I was. I grabbed his shirt, picked him up, and slammed him against his locker. After the second slam, a teacher grabbed us and pulled us into his empty classroom. He asked me what this was all about and I told him. He turned to the kid and asked if it was true. He nodded yes. The teacher then said, "Let's go right now down to the gym and get you some gloves. I'll watch over the fight myself" (things were sure different then). The teacher and I stood up to go, but the other kid just sat there. With a sheepish expression and halting speech, he dropped his head and said, "No need. I screwed up." He then turned to me and said, "I'm really sorry, Chris."

So now what? I wasn't a believer at the time, so I only had a cursory understanding of forgiveness. I knew one thing, though: I had to look tough. But then suddenly something happened. I looked over

THE WILD LOVE OF GOD

at him and saw this pathetic look on his face. Instantly I found myself with a certain degree of compassion for him. What's happening to me? Am I going to really forgive him? No, I can't do that. Please, somebody stop me. No, no…yes, yes I can, and I did. Though we never became close (graduation was only a couple of months away), we did become closer. That's what forgiveness does. It builds bridges. Reconciliation will not always happen. Jesus didn't say, "Reconcile," He said, "Forgive."

Forgiveness is a universal truth in every aspect of God's creation, from people, even on down to monkeys. A recent study of primates showed that forgiveness is an important part of their health. Observing a group of primates, their handlers noticed that one larger primate hurt two smaller ones within the group. Both smaller primates walked away and spent some time alone.

One, after a short period of time, returned to the group and even interacted with the larger animal. All quickly received him back into the group. The other stayed away, and even when approached by his friends, would not interact with them. He continued to stay away and soon became very sick with a stomach ailment. Shortly thereafter, he fell gravely ill and died. The other primate who returned lived a long and happy life. Hmm, even monkeys know that forgiveness is a wise way to live.

Although learning the lessons of forgiveness were never easy, they were all necessary steps that had brought me to the place of now extending that very gift to my own father. Unlike my moment in Montreal when I accepted his apology, more for the reason of moving on and enjoying my week, this would be an all-encompassing expression of forgiveness, total and without any expectation on his part.

The gift of forgiveness. It was now time to apply the lessons I'd learned.

The Gift of Forgiveness

———◇◇◇———

IT WAS TIME. *Okay, Lord, here we go.* I interrupted my father mid-sentence and said, "Hey, Dad, can I talk to you a minute?" He stopped what he was saying and simply said, "Sure, what's up?" I had planned a very articulate little speech, but I totally lost track of everything I had planned to say and instead blurted out, "You know everything that happened to me, to us, when I was young?" I had hoped he knew what I was talking about so I wouldn't have to say more. Fortunately, he did.

He hesitated and then slowly and quietly responded, "Yeah." I'm sure he thought I was about to dredge up the past and throw it in his face. But I wasn't. I remembered my little speech, but I knew those words weren't right. That little speech went right out the window.

He was facing the garden, a blank look on his face. I couldn't read him, but I knew I wasn't supposed to. I was just to forgive him. That's the gift. So I said, "I just want you to know that I love you and I forgive you for everything that ever happened."

I waited for him to either erupt or walk away. He did neither. Instead, he stood there and said nothing. That was even worse. He didn't say a word and he didn't move a muscle. I wasn't sure what to do, so I just waited. As I was standing there, I heard a still, small voice say, "Put your arm around him." I wanted to rebuke the voice, but I knew Who it was. I said inside, "No, Lord, please don't make me do that. Let me wait to see what he's going to do." Again I heard, "Put your arm around him." This time I said yes and I extended my arm and put it around him, my right hand finally resting on his right shoulder. I had no idea what to expect.

The moment my hand hit his shoulder, he immediately began to weep. At first it was a soft and gentle cry, but as I held him it became deeper and deeper. Soon his whole body was shaking. I continued to hold him, but suddenly his left hand came up and he put it around my waist, holding onto me as I held onto him. When his hand came around me, I was suddenly filled with compassion and love for him. Instantly, I too, began to cry.

In the middle of a Fourth of July picnic, with everyone standing thirty feet behind us, there stood my dad and I, holding onto each other, weeping like babies. We stayed just like that for another minute, crying and literally holding each other up. After a few more moments, we both began to settle down, neither of us saying a word.

As we stood there dripping wet, I knew that neither of us had anything to wipe our faces with. So I reached up to my face, wiped my eyes, and with a hand full of tears, I pointed to the garden and said, "Look at how high that corn is." My dad laughed, instantly figuring out that I was trying to find a way to wipe our faces before we turned around to the rest of the family. He followed me with a swipe of his hand over his face, pointed to the lettuce and said, "Well, take a look at how big that lettuce is getting." I laughed and a moment later we were going back and forth, wiping our faces clean and making funny comments about the garden.

Finally we felt clean enough and we turned around, gave each other another quick hug, and headed back to the rest of the family. I was never sure if anyone ever saw the exchange between my father and me, but to this day, no one has ever mentioned it. As a matter of fact, my father and I never talked about that moment again. It was a special time, captured forever in our hearts, the hearts of the two who needed it most.

Papa's Kiss

—◦◦◦—

CHAPTER 10

FOR YEARS I HAD BEEN DISTANT AND COLD toward my father. Now suddenly we were not just relating, we were actually enjoying the relationship. We saw each other with new eyes. I now saw a man who had gone through a horrible experience and needed his son's acceptance, and he was now able to see a son who had been hurt and needed to know his father's love. It was finally a perfect fit.

Because of the closeness of our church community, hugging was as common as a handshake. Shortly after our time beside the garden, on a sunny Sunday afternoon, we went straight from church to my father's house for lunch. When he opened the door to have us enter the house, we all walked in and without thinking, I reached out and gave him a big bear hug. We had hugged before, but never like that. He looked at me, and though he was a bit surprised, I could tell he enjoyed it.

When the visit was over and it was time to go, we headed for the door. My father was standing there holding his arms out, waiting for another bear hug. I went over to him and put my arms around him. We held each other a bit longer this time as a new love and a new trust was beginning to grow.

From that time on, whenever we would greet each other, we embraced with great warmth. Thus began a ten-year span of a slow yet deliberate growth in trust and mutual affection. Every time we would arrive at his home, his arms would be opened wide to receive us.

My kids loved his greetings. One of their fondest memories would be as my dad reached down to give them a kiss. He would sometimes take his unshaven face and rub it against their cheeks. They always squirmed and pulled back, but they all told me later that they loved it when he did that.

Something changed in me when I saw him with my children. His tenderness with them showed me what was really inside. When he embraced them, I was able to also take it for myself. He could still be a little surly (just ask his stepchildren), but he was growing toward wholeness and kindness.

As time passed, I was invited back to a Catholic community that I had visited back in the seventies. It was in a beautiful country setting outside the city of Albany, New York. When I arrived for the week's activity, I was greeted by a gentleman who, instead of a handshake or a hug, greeted me with a kiss upon the cheek.

This kind of threw me for a moment and he noticed my awkward look. He looked at me and said, "Sorry if I just made you uncomfortable, but we believe in the importance of an honorable greeting. As it says in Romans 16:16, 'Greet one another with a holy kiss.'"

For the next few days I was inundated with people kissing me on the cheek. It was uncomfortable at first, but after a couple of days, I began to get used to it. By the end of the week, I found myself not only feeling at ease with the situation, I was becoming a kisser. I was probably kissing dogs and trees by the time the week was over.

I drove back on a Saturday, and after church on Sunday, we took off for my father's house. Upon arriving, I fell into his arms. But instead of just a hug, without even thinking, I planted a big kiss on his right cheek. I couldn't believe it. I had just kissed my father.

He stepped back and stared at me. I didn't think he'd be mad, but I wasn't sure what he was thinking. Suddenly he smiled and said, "I like that." He then walked over to me and planted a big kiss on my right cheek. He then said, "Yep, I like that. Let's do that all the time." And so we did.

There was always a father's kiss when we said hello or said good-bye. Every kiss seemed to wash my soul, giving me not just greater affection for him, but releasing even greater affection for my own children. I was beginning to realize how deeply affection creates an empowered heart. We love because we're loved.

As time passed, for the first time in my life, I began to look forward to being with my dad. I'd never had that feeling before and it was a wonderful thing to feel.

I remember coming down his street one day and I noticed that the drapes to his front window were pulled back. As we came near the house, I saw the drapes fall.

As we pulled into the driveway, my father came out the front door and made a beeline for the car. By the time I was turning the car off, my dad had the door open and was pulling me out of the car. He hugged me, kissed my cheek, and then escorted us into the house.

When we entered the house, his wife, Marian, pulled me aside.

She said, "Your dad has been at the window for almost an hour. When I asked him why he was standing there, he said, 'I can't wait to see Chris.'"

She asked him why, and with a sly smile he said, "I just want to kiss his face."

"I just want to kiss his face." I loved those words. Life continued with lightness in our relationship that carried us through the years. There were moments that would test this new season, but they were few and far between.

Almost ten years after our moment in the garden, my father called and asked if I could come over. I jumped in the car and went straight to his place. When he opened the door, there was a soberness to him that I hadn't seen in a long time. He led me into the living room and asked me to sit down. He pulled out a large sleeve that I knew contained x-rays. He handed me the sleeve and asked me to pull out the x-ray that was inside.

I pulled out the x-ray and put it up to some light. I had seen many x-rays over the years working as a surgical technician, but I had never seen one that looked like this. It was a chest x-ray, but instead of a localized area where there may be a tumor or anything specific, the entire x-ray looked like it was encased in fog. There was just a big gray area that covered the whole thing. You could make out the lungs, but it was like looking through a filter.

He said that the doctor did not know what was going on, and that he, my father, would need to come into the hospital so a small sample of the lung could be taken through a simple out-patient procedure done under local anesthesia. The moment he said that,

I heard this still, small voice inside me say, "Go with your father whenever he has to go to the doctor or to the hospital." Okay, I had my marching orders.

I first went to his follow-up doctor's appointment and again heard that no one was quite sure what was going on with my dad. The doctor hemmed and hawed, but would not land on or commit to anything solid. I understood why, but after a while he did talk about the possibility that it might be cancer. We asked for a prognosis, but he only gave a vague answer, as he really didn't know what was ailing my father. He set the next day as the day to come in for the outpatient procedure.

I picked up my father early the next morning and we drove to the hospital. I could tell that he was nervous. He asked what the procedure was like and I told him.

He then said, "Sorry I asked."

I said, "Don't be nervous, Dad. It will be over very quickly."

He then told me that he wasn't nervous about the procedure; he was nervous about what they would find. We prayed as we pulled into the hospital parking lot. It was so nice to be connected to his heart.

After we found the outpatient surgical area, Dad got all dressed up in his best hospital garb. Being the no-nonsense guy that he was, he walked out of the bathroom like he owned the place and headed straight for me. He looked a little too "breezy," so I had him turn around. Sure enough, there he was, two cheeks to the wind—a free show for everyone in the waiting room. I helped tie him off in the back.

After a short wait, they called his name and we both got up. I asked if I could be seated near his head during the procedure. Because it was under local anesthesia and they knew me from working in surgery, they had no problem with my being there.

The procedure began normally, but I soon realized that they were having trouble getting a specimen from his lung. Each attempt was bringing my dad more needle pricks, more trocar invasions, and always more pain. Finally after what seemed like forever, they stopped and gave up. "That's enough trauma for one day, Mr. DuPré," the doctor said. "I'm sorry we could not get what we needed. It doesn't appear we will if we continue to go through this way. We'll have to reschedule you to return and use another entry point."

My dad whispered to me, "Wow, now that's some great news." I started laughing as did the doctor who heard his loud whisper. My dad was then sent back to change, and we left the hospital with an appointment for the following week.

I again picked him up for the following week's procedure. This time, though, he looked a bit more nervous. Knowing what he had experienced the week before, I couldn't blame him. I tried to reassure him that it would be better this time. He told me that the procedure was not what he was nervous about.

He then confessed to me that his greatest fear would be that he would be diagnosed with lung cancer and that as it would metastasize, he would slowly and painfully suffocate. My dad always wore larger shirts so the collar would not press against his neck, especially when he wore ties. Also when he'd get his hair cut, he would always get covered in hair because he never wanted the cape to be tightened around his neck. I was aware of all this, but suddenly things made sense. He hated the feeling of being choked, and death by suffocating would be the worst possible way for him to go. We prayed right then and there that his greatest fear would never come to pass.

The hospital visit this time brought forth an identical scenario as the week before. They tried another entry point, more needle pricks, more trocars invading his body, more pain, and in the end, the same result. No specimen. I had a funny feeling what they would say next, and I was right.

After the procedure, we met with the doctor and he said that the only way he could probably get a specimen would be to do what's called a lung biopsy. It was a fairly simple procedure where the doctor makes a small incision in the chest, cuts through to the ribs, separates two of them, and puts a long thin instrument down to get a small specimen of the lung. The reason it hadn't been done up to this point was that a lung biopsy was done under general anesthesia instead of local anesthesia.

The doctor gave my father about a week to heal up after the second attempt under local anesthesia and then quickly went ahead and scheduled him for a lung biopsy.

Marian took dad to the hospital on the appointed day and I met them there. I entered his room and found him sitting on the edge of his bed. His shirt was off and his upper body was covered with red blotches. I saw the blotches and was concerned. I hid it well and went right to him.

I hugged him, and shortly after that, someone came to take him to surgery. Because they knew me, they let me wheel him down to the surgical holding room. Marian followed as we went. We entered the holding room and were introduced to the holding room nurse. Her job was to make sure she had the right patient going in for the right procedure. Everything checked out and we found a spot to park the stretcher.

About fifteen minutes later, a nurse entered and called his name. Dad lifted his hand and she came over. She was the circulating nurse, the nurse in charge of keeping things running smoothly in the surgical room. She came over and went through the same ordeal the holding room nurse had gone through earlier. Very thorough and very professional.

As she was finishing, a hoard of masked men in green scrubs came through the door. Out front was the attending physician, the doctor in charge of performing the surgery. He was followed by a surgical resident, the anesthesiologist, and a third-year medical student. A veritable wall of green.

The attending surgeon (an excellent doctor I had worked with many times over the years) introduced everyone on the team to Marian and me and told my father it was time to say goodbye to us. Marian leaned over and gave him a kiss. I, too embarrassed to kiss him, put my right hand into the stretcher and gave him a "cool guy" handshake.

My father looked at me like I was nuts. He said, "Oh, no, that won't do." He then proceeded to pull my hand, dragging my body over the edge of the stretcher. By the time he stopped pulling, I was almost fully into the stretcher, just barely dangling on one of my toes. The doctors had started to move, but instead stopped to watch the action.

My dad took my face and held it in both his hands. He looked at me, and then pulled my face towards his, kissing me on both cheeks. I quickly lost my "cool" and let myself enjoy the moment. He then pulled my head back and turned it so that I faced the surgical team. I will never forget this moment as I was forever changed in the following seconds. With great pride and love, he looked right at the team and said, "This is my son. I love him."

I was stunned, as was the surgical team. They didn't quite know what to do. They nodded, looked at each other, and began to head out. My dad turned back to me and then said, "Nope, that's not good enough." Not quite knowing what that meant, the surgical team turned around again and stopped.

My father mouthed out the words, "I love you," to me and then one last time, he pulled my face toward his and kissed me. I was in heaven. My father, totally unashamed of me, his son, lavishing me with kisses. He let me go, turned to the nurse and said, "Okay, now I'm ready."

They started wheeling him toward the elevators, which were about thirty feet away. But before they could even go ten feet, my father yelled, "Stop!" The nurse thought something was wrong and stopped the stretcher right away. Once again, the surgical team stopped in their tracks. The nurse asked, "What's wrong, Mr. Du-Pré?" My father answered, "I can't see my son when you wheel me in this direction. Please turn me around." She turned to me and smiled. I also smiled as my eyes began to fill with tears.

She turned him around and then began to pull him toward the elevators. He was now facing me and Marian. I blew him a kiss and he blew one back. Then he started a series of kisses that had the room laughing. He blew a kiss, loaded an imaginary gun, and shot me with kisses, kissed his finger and tweaked it to me, and then went back to blowing me more kisses. In between kisses he was signing, "I love you," with his hands. The surgical team just stood there, mesmerized. I must admit; they were fun to watch.

Finally, the stretcher arrived at the elevator. The doors opened and the nurse began to pull him in. He was in the center of the elevator, but the door was closing from his right to his left. As the door began to close, he shifted in his stretcher, leaned over the left edge of the stretcher and blew me one last kiss, ending with his thumb of approval raised high in the air, and a big smile splashed across his face. The doors closed and he was on his way.

The surgical team looked at me, awkwardly smiled, turned and walked away. The nurse in the holding room came over to me and said, "I have never seen anything like that before. I love to see a father who loves his children." Holding back tears, I was able to quietly say, "Me too."

Marian and I headed for the surgical waiting room. Knowing it was about an hour-long surgery, I grabbed a newspaper and sat down. I found it hard to concentrate on what was in front of me. I was still enjoying the high of being loved on by my father. Sitting there gave me time to drink it all in. It also gave me time to think.

I had recently been studying Luke 15, the chapter about the prodigal son. As I did, I realized that the prodigal son was just one of many characters in the chapter. The story is really about the father. The younger son, humbled by his prodigal ways, returns home broke, having wasted his precious inheritance. Not knowing what the father would do, he returns anyway, hoping against hope that maybe he would be able to enter back in, even if he had to return as a servant. At least that way he'd get something to eat.

As he shuffles up the road, his father sees him from afar. My thoughts drifted back to my own dad, standing at the window with the curtain pulled back, waiting for me to arrive so that he could run out and give me a kiss. "I just want to kiss his face."

The father in Luke 15 was waiting, too. He was waiting to lavish love and kisses upon his son—not a love dependent upon the son's obedience, but a love based upon the father's goodness. There's a huge difference.

The moment the father sees his son he takes off. I have this feeling that when the son saw his father he got very nervous. The culture at the time permitted women, children, and slaves to run, but it was a shame for men to run unless they were going into battle. Was his father going into battle? Against him? Whatever the son thought, he decided to stay and not run. He would live or die in his father's presence.

As the father got closer, the son must have seen his smile. He must have seen the joy over his father's face, dispelling any thoughts of battle. When his father reached him, the first thing he did was to "fall on his neck and kiss him." This word for *kiss* here is a present progressive verb that means, "to kiss and kiss and keep on kissing."

As he was kissed over and over, shame was being lifted off and removed from his soul.

I knew how that son felt. I had just been kissed by my own father over and over, and I saw the joy on my father's face. Sitting there waiting for the surgery to be over gave me time to pray, but also time to bask in the love that my father had just lavished upon me.

After we'd been there a little over an hour, they called our name and we were asked to go to a small conference room. As we waited for the doctor, Marian was asking me what would happen if they found out he had cancer. She and I hadn't specifically talked about that up to this point, and she began to share how hard it would be to know she had only a year or two left with my dad.

We talked for a few minutes. I tried to be encouraging, but whatever I said didn't seem to bring her much peace. In the middle of an emotional moment, the doctor very stoically walked in, followed closely by the anesthesiologist. I did not take this as a good sign. I wondered why the anesthesiologist was with the doctor.

They again introduced themselves. We sat down and waited to hear what they found. Was he okay or did he have cancer, and if so, what was his prognosis? Without hesitation or emotion, they said what neither of us was expecting. The attending surgeon looked back and forth between me and Marian, finally settling on the space between us and said, "I'm sorry to have to tell you this, but Mr. DuPré passed away on the table shortly after we got started. We did all we could to revive him, but it was of no use. Again, I'm so sorry."

Instantly Marian let out a blood-curdling scream and collapsed into my lap. She began to weep uncontrollably. I put my arms around her and held her tightly, fighting off my own tears. The doctors sat there and let us take in the news. After a short time, I asked what had happened. He said that they felt it was a blood clot that was trapped between the heart and the lungs, called a pulmonary embolism.

I looked at the anesthesiologist and said, "I noticed how blotchy my father was this morning. Did he get enough fluids before surgery?" He looked at me like I had shot him in the chest. He hesitated for a moment and then said, "That's a question I've been asking myself. I believe he did. I feel as if we did everything we could do."

I appreciated his honesty. The attending surgeon then said, "We could order an autopsy if you'd like to determine the exact cause of death, but I think you need to know one thing. When we opened Mr. DuPré's chest cavity, we found no specific tumor. Instead, the entire chest cavity was filled with cancer. It covered every area. To be honest with you, I don't understand how he's been alive for so long."

Marian began to lift herself up and then said, "I don't want an autopsy. He's been cut up enough." I then asked the doctor, "If my father had lived through this surgery, what would have happened to him? What would have been his prognosis?" He looked at me with steel eyes and said, "He would have died within the next few months. Basically, it would have choked him from within. To be brutally honest with you, it would have been a horrible way to die."

I realized at that moment, my father's death, though one of the most painful moments of my life, was a gift for him. Instead of experiencing his greatest fear, that of choking to death, he quietly went to sleep and woke up face to face with Jesus. Instead of a horribly painful, dragged out death, he lavished love upon his family and then quietly and peacefully slipped into eternity.

I also then realized the precious gift that I had just received that day. Instead of a quick goodbye, like I almost gave my father, he gave me the gift of extravagant affection. I now have embedded in my memory a father declaring his love for me, not out of duty, but out of desire.

It became a living example for me of the face-to-face encounter I'd had years earlier with Jesus. I saw the face of love, Wild Love. A love that was not under man's control. A love that was unashamed and full of passion. That day, my father gave me a gift for which I will be forever grateful. Thank you, Papa. I look forward to seeing you again, face to face.

The usual events followed. We met with a local funeral home and scheduled two days of showings. The funeral director questioned the need for two days, but we reassured him that it would be needed. We headed back to Marian's house to gather as a family. My job was to call a list of relatives. I placed some calls, each one bringing the pain of his death back to life.

As I was getting ready to make another call, the phone rang. I picked it up and said, "Hello." The man on the other end heard my voice and said, "Oh thank God, Dave. I heard that you had died. It's so good to hear your voice." I couldn't speak for a moment. The voice then said, "Hello...Dave, are you there?" I slowly answered him, "I'm so sorry, but this is his son, Chris. I hate to have to tell you this but my father did pass away this morning." I don't recall any more of that conversation. I do remember after talking to him that I sat there for quite a while in a daze. From then on, every time I answered the phone, I gave my name out first.

The wake went well—as well as wakes can go. The funeral director said that he couldn't remember when so many people had been at his funeral home. Part way through the second night he said that we should have booked three days instead of two. We all laughed.

The local congresswoman came, as did many of the city's dignitaries. Because of my dad's involvement with the Veteran's Administration, he was kind of like a local hero to area vets. They showed up in large numbers, as did many of his former students. Over and over again I heard, "Your dad was my favorite teacher." The joy for me was that I no longer responded negatively in my heart. I was able to rejoice with them and celebrate the man who was my father. It was an emotional two days, but also a very warm and memorable two days.

The day after the wake we had a church funeral service followed by his burial at a local cemetery. Because he was a veteran, he was given a military service, complete with a twenty-one-gun salute. It was very moving for all and we left there saddened at the loss, but now able to more clearly see the greatness of the man. Not perfect by any means, but with his passing, the fruit of his life came out from the shadows and everyone got to see the impact he'd had on thousands of lives. Somehow I felt that I was near the top of that list.

CHAPTER 11

The Gift
Continues

——⟡⟡⟡——

O N THAT FATEFUL DAY in June of 1991, my father went in for surgery, was gently put to sleep, and never again awakened to this world. He was now in another world, face to face with Jesus.

Less than a year after my father's death, my mother began to feel ill. This was nothing new as over the years I had seen my mother go through one physical battle after another. When I was little, I remember her going to the doctor quite often.

I think I learned about the human body through whatever operation or procedure was next. What's a thyroid? It needs to come out. Where is your gall bladder? That goes too. Why does a bad heart make you run out of breath? We'll leave your heart in there but give you some medication for it. My mother had always had a shelf of pills in the house that would put a pharmacy to shame.

Was she a hypochondriac? I don't know. As a child, that's not a question you ask. You might think it, but you'd never talk about it. What I do know is that when she began to talk about her pain this time, something seemed to be different. She went into the hospital through the emergency room. I met her there and the doctor said that she was experiencing some kind of bowel discomfort. They said she might be battling diverticulitis, a painful condition where inflammation occurs in the wall of the colon, usually within the large intestine.

They admitted her and began to treat her. After a short time, they decided that if she continued with her daily medications, she could be released to go home. She took her new medications, but instead of going back to her apartment where she would be alone, she ended up going to my brother's house to stay close to family. It was a painful time for her, and after a short period of time, she ended up back in the hospital. It turned out that she had a horribly aggressive case of Crohn's disease.

Because she had been treated for other problems, the Crohn's disease had spread like wildfire. They did a temporary colostomy on her and flooded her with new medication. When I visited her, she was stable. She told me not to worry and that she would be fine.

Soon after, I received a call from a friend in Kansas City who was looking for a seventh grade teacher. I had taught junior high for four years, so I flew out, had an interview, and was hired on the spot. I now had a new job in a new city.

Shortly after our move to Kansas City, my sister called to say that mom was not getting better. On the contrary, she was going downhill. The Crohn's disease had spread throughout her small and large intestine and they would have to remove everything. She would have to receive radiation treatments as well as possibly chemo just to extend her life for one to two years. She decided to keep herself intact and not be carved up, radiated, and fed through a tube just to live a little longer.

When school started, I arrived and attended the first day of faculty-only meetings. After a few hours, I received a call at school about my mother. I was told that she was dying and that if I wanted to see her, I needed to come as soon as possible. I was excused and headed back to Rochester.

What I saw when I entered her room was a very different Mary Kay DuPré than the one I had seen a few months before. Her face was gaunt, her skin was clammy, and her coloring was as white as could be. I held back tears and went right over to hug her. Her arms felt very weak and yet they surrounded me with increased strength as we hugged. We both knew why I was there—to say goodbye.

I pulled a chair up to her bed and she asked how things were going in Kansas City. We talked for a while and then she dozed off. When she awakened, she was suddenly very energetic. It was as if she knew our time was short and she wanted to make the most of it.

After a short time of talking, she put her hand up near my mouth and with her index finger, touched the mustache that had been on my lip for twenty years. She looked at me and said, "I always loved your face. Could I see it one more time without the hair?" Before those words even fell to the floor, I stood up, walked into her bathroom, found the ugly plastic razor that was there, soaped up my mustache, and shaved it off.

I walked back out and again sat down next to her. She put her hand back up and stroked my lip. "There, that's the lovely face I remember. That's my baby." I started to cry and she patted my face. "It's okay, Chris. I love Him and I'll see Him soon." Through my tears I said, "I know, Mom. I'm just gonna miss you." Someone came in to measure some reading and the moment passed. We talked some more until she once again became tired, and then I left for the day.

When I came in the next day, she was sitting up with a look that said, "Hey, let's talk." She knew what we had gone through as a family years before, but she didn't know how much I really knew as I was the youngest. I assured her that I knew much less than she and that anything she could tell me about when I was young would be of great value to me.

So for the next three days, she poured out her heart (in between doctors, nurses, and other visitors) and told me things that I had never heard before. She talked of her marriage to my dad and the breakdown that happened over the years. She talked about the multiple separations that they had gone through and how, as she put it, it was a miracle that I was ever born, let alone conceived.

She led me through each year of my life, helping me put the pieces into place. I wish I had recorded it, but knowing my mother, she would never have let me, or if she did, she would have only given a very watered-down version.

By our final day together, we had bonded in a way that had never happened before. She was passing me a baton of knowledge that I was now to carry. I realized that she had carried an enormous weight over the years and it had taken its toll. She felt lighter and looked lighter, and I knew that she was ready to go to Jesus.

I headed back to my brother's house. As my brother and I talked about my time with Mom, I realized that in spite of all the pain my mother had gone through, she was clean in her heart toward my dad. I also realized that this day had been a test for me, too. I knew I had forgiven my dad for what he had done to me, but I now found myself continuing to forgive him for what he had done to my mother.

That was a revelation for me. Forgiving my father for what he had done to me was a good first step, but for forgiveness to be complete, I would need to forgive him for how he had also hurt those whom I most loved. That realization turned a light on for me. From this point on, I would need to be making sure that forgiveness was ongoing, not just toward my dad, but toward every person in my life—past, present, and future. God has always been very intentional in His forgiveness; I also needed to do the same.

The next morning I headed over to the hospital. I only had a short time as I had to catch a plane. As the moment came for me to leave, I sat on the edge of her bed and just held her hand. She looked at me and smiled, a tear coming down one of her cheeks.

She lifted up her hand and once again touched my lip. "My baby boy," she said, over and over. Finally, we hugged a big, long hug, and then she held me at arms length. "Now, you have a wonderful trip home," she said. With my eyes filled with tears, I looked at her and said, "You too, Mom. Have a wonderful trip home."

We hugged once more and I got up, blew her a kiss, and began to walk out of the room. I held in most of my tears until I was mid-way down the hallway, and then the dam burst. With people all around, I wept like a baby, walking and weeping right out of the hospital. I walked down the street to my brother's house and waited outside until the flow of tears had ended. I caught a flight back to Kansas City later that day.

The following week on the first day of school, I received a call that my mother had just died. I instantly saw her in His Presence and felt both loss and joy. I would never see her again in this life, but I knew she was finally without pain. I went back to the classroom and finished out the day with the knowledge that she was seeing the One she loved the most, face to face. She was finally experiencing the look of Wild Love.

Wild Love

—◦◦◦—

IT'S BEEN YEARS SINCE MY FATHER passed away, but not a day goes by that I don't remember his look of affection toward me. His look and his gift of Wild Love are forever burned upon my heart. You see, that's what it's all about: Really seeing the heart that's behind the eyes. My father spent many years as an angry and lonely man, and yet he is remembered by most as a man filled with life and love.

It's not always how we start the race—it's how we finish. My father finished well. That's what's so wonderful about our gracious Father. We can let yesterday go and begin all over again. He throws our sins into a sea of forgetfulness and chooses to remember them no longer. We, on the other hand, usually have a much harder time letting our sins and weaknesses go. We hold tightly onto what God has already forgotten. We are often our own worst enemies.

Forgiveness is just the beginning, though. Yes, we all need to cultivate a life of forgiveness—forgiveness of ourselves and of others. But once we've tasted His grace and forgiveness, we need to move on to the heart behind that grace and really know the Person behind the forgiveness. We constantly receive His many gifts of grace throughout our lives, but we become trapped in the cycle of knowing *about* Him and yet never really *knowing* Him. It's like reading book after book about a very famous person. We become experts in the minutia concerning them but we've never gazed into their eyes and seen what's truly inside.

I sometimes want to remove the tag "Christian" from people so they can forget about being a part of a "group" and remember that all God ever wanted to do with man was walk with him in the Garden. He didn't desire denominations or factions; He has always been after desiring to convince the human heart that He is good and He is crazy about us.

I hope you're not offended by my use of the word *crazy*. I mean that in its purest sense. One of the more informal definitions for *crazy* is "being over the top in love, which produces an extreme passion." What's more extreme than to leave the glories of heaven, become a man, suffer the worst form of death imaginable, die and be buried, all because you are in love with someone. That someone is me and that someone is you.

That's what makes His love for us a Wild Love. It is a love that is unrestrained by human hands. No man can or ever will control who God loves or how deeply He loves. If we, as Christians, think that our religious systems funnel or have a control valve on how God thinks or feels about us, we are deceived. If I am part of something that makes people question God's love for them, I am doing the enemy's work.

I'm not talking about the importance of wisdom issues or having people in our lives that can speak to the deepest level of our hearts. I'm talking about church structures that we at first built to bring needed order, and yet over time, those pillars of order have more power in our lives than the tender voice of the One who gave His life for us.

Jesus said that we weren't made for the Sabbath, the Sabbath was made for us (see Mark 2:27). In like manner, we weren't made for the Church, the Church (that is, the idea of a people who gather together, with all its inherent goodness and weakness) was made for us. People were not made to meet the needs of a church. We were made for Him. We were made for love.

What is your identity? Are you a Christian? Okay, that's a great start, but that in and of itself is not God's main identity for you. It's a label we have created to identify Who we believe is God. That's not wrong, but it doesn't automatically create lovers of God.

Proverbs 23:7 says that as a man thinks in his heart, so is he. What we believe, specifically about the nature of God, determines how we think. How we think determines what we do. As believers, do we have within us an identity that carries us through life? If not, we become slaves to, or even worse, victims of every emotion and circumstance that surrounds us. That is not our destiny.

Years ago the Lord whispered to me, "Who are you?" When God asks you a question, He's not asking because He doesn't know something. I did not answer Him right away. Instead I went to the One Who would know best. I asked Him. "Okay, Lord, who am I?" His answer confirmed my journey and once and for all set my heart in a secure and immovable place. He simply said this: "You are a loved son."

I'm a loved son! Yes, I'm a loved son! That's it. Everything else makes sense after that. As a loved son, I am secure in my Father's love. That love is not dependent on my goodness or faithfulness; it comes from His goodness and His faithfulness. I'm not held by my promises to God; I'm upheld by God's promises to me.

Therefore, as a loved son, I can become a more loving husband. As a loved son, I make a more gracious and patient father. As a loved son, I'm a more faithful friend. As the saying goes, "My roots determine my fruit." Ephesians 3:17 says that I must be "rooted and grounded in love," in order that I may, as verses 18 and 19 say, "comprehend with all the saints what is the width and length and depth and height—to know the love of Christ."

Did you catch that? We need to know His love in order to comprehend His love. That means my main objective in life is not to prove my love to Him, but to know His love for me. I love because He first loved me. I can only love to the extent I know I'm loved.

It may appear selfish in print... "I'm gonna put God loving me first on my list," yet when done as a lifestyle based upon relationship, people experience the fruit of your walk, not the sound of your talk. They experience His love through you, not the secret life of His love coming to you.

A heart that knows the Father's affection is a heart at rest. No longer is performance the driving force of life. People at rest have nothing to prove. Nothing I can do will affect His affection for me or change His love to me. My love, my obedience, my very life, turns from becoming my Christian duty and instead becomes what it was meant to be: a response of a heart overflowing with love. Freely received, freely given. There's nothing more pure than when love is freely given, no strings attached.

Immediately after I was saved, I was ushered into a community where worship was the top priority. A wonderful atmosphere was present time and time again as we gathered to sing and worship the Lord. It wasn't long, though, before "good teaching" and the importance of "well-crafted services" replaced the simple devotion that was at first present. As this shift was taking place, I wrote a song that expressed the confusion I had in my heart. The first couple of verses went like this:

> Where do I go from here?
> I'm just a babe I need some help now.
> You've been this way before.
> Where do I go?

> Where do I go from here?
> You say He speaks, how does one listen?
> You've heard His voice I know.
> Where do I go?

That became my cry. *Lord, where do I go? Where do I aim the rocket of my heart?* He came to me, face to face and showed me that I was to pursue His Wild Love. That was my answer then, and that's still His invitation now. As the years go by and I find myself a father and now a grandfather, my main mission and goal of life has never changed. Because I'm first loved, I love. It's so simple. As the expression goes, *even a child can do it.*

As I've shared the story of my father over the years, I've found so many people who deeply ache for some kind of resolve with their own earthly father. There were never any words of love between them and their father, and they see no hope. For others, their father passed away years before and they realize they'll never be able to be restored to their dad.

So, where do they go from here? They go to the same One who longs to be face to face with them. My journey is not meant to be duplicated. Our testimonies are never meant to be shared in order to boast or to set people up to think that what happened to me will happen to them. Too many are disappointed with that kind of thinking.

Our stories are meant to inspire others to find God and know Him themselves. I'm not here to live out someone else's promises. I'm here to know Him and hear for myself what He has in store for me. That takes time and that takes relationship. We will dig deeper in that relationship, though, if our hearts are convinced that He is for us and that He actually does like us. He is right there waiting for us to accept His Wild Love.

When I was living in Rochester, my youngest daughter came up to me and asked if she could talk to me. She was probably four at the time. I said I'd love to talk, so I lifted her up and put her on my lap. I asked her about her day, and she told me a few things about hers. But soon enough, she started to yawn. A few minutes later she was sound asleep. I just looked at her and marveled at how beautiful she was. I found myself focused on her little toes. They were so cute. They were so chewable I wanted to eat them up. Laura came into the room and I called her over. I said, "Look at her toes. I love these toes."

Years later we were living in Kansas City. I was being challenged in the disciplines of my Christian walk and, feeling a little insecure, I felt that God was unhappy with my prayer life. I was determined to do better, so I set my alarm early to seek Him at daybreak. The alarm went off and I pulled myself away from my den of warm blankets and slid to my knees next to the bed. I leaned over onto the bed and start to pray. About forty-five minutes later, I woke up in a puddle of drool. Not only had I not prayed, but I fell asleep, right there in His Presence. I was ashamed of myself.

As I knelt there I heard His unmistakable voice. It was so clear. It was as if someone was speaking out loud right there in the room. He said, "I love your toes. I just love those toes." I didn't have a clue what was going on. I knelt there for a moment, and then it hit me. Though it was over five years earlier, I had done the same thing with my daughter. She had come to me in order to spend time with me and yet, despite her best intentions, she fell asleep in my presence. All I could remember was how beautiful she was and how much I loved her, and her cute little toes.

And now, here I was, trying to impress Him with my new prayer life, and I fall asleep. Only His response was not one of disappointment, it was one of celebrating who I was to Him. While I was "out of it," He was looking at my toes. He was enjoying me. That's what He does.

Oh, but Chris, you don't know me. I hear that all the time. You see, I don't need to know you; I know Him. I'm not saying you can go ahead and make bad choices and His love for you will automatically remove every negative consequence. We reap what we sow. We need to know His Word and His ways, and we need to walk in wisdom. That's also a part of love.

But this I also know: He sees our desire to be with Him. We don't always follow up like we'd like to, but He sees our hearts and how we really do long for Him. Again, I'm not advocating a lazy life in God, but I am advocating an honest evaluation of how He sees us. We're His kids. He loves His kids. He loves your toes. Even that funny one that turns out to the side. He is in love with you.

A few years later I was sitting in my living room playing a David Ruis song, "We Will Dance on the Streets that are Golden." I love that song and used it often while leading worship. My youngest daughter came into the living room, sat next to me, and started to sing with me. She's got a beautiful voice and has a natural gift to sing harmony. I was thoroughly enjoying it.

Suddenly she got up and went to her room. I kept playing, but was sad that she left. A few minutes later she walked out of her room dressed in her dance whites. She'd been dancing since she was little and was a wonderfully graceful dancer. She began to dance around the room, lifting a delicate white veil that hung in the air like a sweet perfume. As she danced, I was caught off guard. I started to tear up. My daughter was dancing unashamed before her father. It doesn't get any better than that.

A few minutes into the song I realized that although I wanted to join the billions dancing on the streets that are golden, at this moment, all I wanted to do was see one person dance—my daughter. A moment later I heard His voice again. He gently said, "That's how I feel about you. I love the multitudes, but I also love the one. I love to just be with you."

Tears filled my eyes as I heard His affection for me and watched my daughter worship Him in the dance. A few minutes later as the song was supposed to end, I kept playing and found myself singing something else. Within a few minutes a whole new song emerged, one that for me was birthed out of one of the most personal and intimate times I've ever had with Him.

This simple song has gone on to be sung by many who have shared a similar testimony with me. As they've sung this song, God has brought healing to their hearts and helped them strip away a false image of a harsh and cold Father. They have gone on to feel His embrace and know that He desires to hold them and spend the rest of their lives dancing in His arms of love.

Dance with me

O Lover of my soul

To the Song of all Songs

Romance me

O Lover of my soul

To the Song of all Songs

Behold You have come

Over the hills

Upon the mountains

To me You have run

My Beloved, You're captured my heart

With You I will go

For You are my love

You are my fair one

> The winter is past
> And the springtime has come

So, where do we go from here? I think we really only have one choice: We move toward Wild Love. Not just move toward it, dive into it with all we have and all we are.

We run to Him because He is safe and because He is good.

We stay near Him because He holds the words to eternal life.

We press into Him because He is love.

We let Him hold us. If we do, one day, sooner or later, we will take the time to look—really look—into His eyes and see what it is we've always needed, what we've always wanted: eyes that look back to us and tell us without words that we are perfectly and completely loved. And when you're captured by His Wild Love, you're captured forever.

THE WILD LOVE OF GOD

—⟨୧୨୧⟩—

The questions in this discussion guide are here to help stir up your own thoughts concerning how you see God and how you think and feel He sees you. How you think determines how you act, and truth searched for and found is always the greatest of treasures.

So whether your go through these questions by yourself or with a small group, remember that God's love is not based upon you and your ability to do or say the right thing. It is based upon Who He is. He doesn't just extend love, He is Love! Enjoy Him as He enjoys you. He loves your little toes!

Chapter 1: David's Story

1. Like my father during WWII, has God ever spared your life, and if so, how?

2. What experience has helped your faith become more personal?

3. What challenges in life did your parents have prior to becoming parents?

—⟡—

_____

_____

_____

_____

_____

_____

_____

_____

_____

_____

_____

_____

_____

_____

_____

_____

_____

_____

_____

Chapter 2: The Return of a War Hero

1. Have you ever had to deal with abuse, and if so, how has it affected your life?

2. Who has been there to protect and/or rescue you?

3. Have you ever sensed that God was protecting you, and if so, how?

Chapter 3: In my Father's House

1. Do you feel you have been labeled by your abilities or lack of abilities? Describe.

2. Because of any labeling, do you think there are any undiscovered gifts within you? If so, what other gifts do you think God has given you?

3. Do you find yourself constantly comparing yourself with others? If so, how does that affect your daily life?

—◦◦◦—

_____

_____

_____

_____

_____

_____

_____

_____

_____

_____

_____

_____

_____

_____

_____

Chapter 4: School Daze

1. Have you ever felt like a dream was taken away from you? If so, how did you respond?

2. How do you handle disappointment?

3. How do you think God feels when your heart is hurting?

———◦◦◦———

_____

_____

_____

_____

_____

_____

_____

_____

_____

_____

_____

_____

_____

_____

_____

_____

_____

_____

_____

_____

Chapter 5: A New Song

1. What do you remember about the first time you heard of Jesus? What helped you move from knowing only *about* Jesus to having a more *personal* relationship with Him?

2. How did God reveal Himself to you and how does He usually speak to you?

3. Have you ever had what you felt was a God-inspired dream?

_____

_____

_____

_____

_____

_____

_____

_____

_____

_____

_____

_____

_____

_____

_____

_____

_____

Chapter 6: Face to Face

1. What do you feel—really feel—is the expression on God's face when He looks at you?

2. Have you ever had a supernatural experience? If so, describe it.

3. What area in your heart do you want God to heal?

———

_____

_____

_____

_____

_____

_____

_____

_____

_____

_____

_____

_____

_____

_____

_____

_____

_____

_____

Chapter 7: Knowing the Father's Heart

1. Have you struggled with your view of God the Father? If so, how?

2. How has your view of someone changed (either positively or negatively) because you saw them through someone else's eyes?

3. Do you feel your life in God is rooted in love, in spiritual activity, or in something else? Describe your answer.

———⟋⟋⟋———

_____

_____

_____

_____

_____

_____

_____

_____

_____

_____

_____

_____

_____

_____

_____

_____

_____

Chapter 8: The Journey of Forgiveness

1. Without using any names, describe an incident in which you needed to forgive someone.

2. Are there people you have forgiven and yet there is still pain in your heart toward them?

3. Are there people you have not yet forgiven? Can you forgive them now?

———

_____

_____

_____

_____

_____

_____

_____

_____

_____

_____

_____

_____

_____

_____

_____

_____

_____

Chapter 9: The Gift of Forgiveness

1. Have you ever told someone face to face that you have forgiven them?

2. Have you been restored to someone because of forgiveness? How did that happen?

3. How does it make you feel when someone forgives you?

—◦◦◦—

_____

_____

_____

_____

_____

_____

_____

_____

_____

_____

_____

_____

_____

_____

_____

_____

_____

_____

Chapter 10: Papa's Kiss

1. Has someone close to you passed away? If so, how did you handle that situation?

2. Is there someone in your life right now whose passing would be more difficult because of a breach in your relationship?

3. What relationships in your life right now could you strengthen if you chose to?

———

_____

_____

_____

_____

_____

_____

_____

_____

_____

_____

_____

_____

_____

_____

_____

_____

_____

Chapter 11: The Gift Continues

1. Which is easier for you—forgiving someone for personally hurting you, or forgiving someone who hurt another person you love? Why?

2. Have you ever had to say a "last goodbye" to someone? Describe the incident.

3. Do you have peace about where you'll be spending eternity? Why or why not?

—◊◊◊—

_____

_____

_____

_____

_____

_____

_____

_____

_____

_____

_____

_____

_____

_____

_____

Chapter 12: Wild Love

1. Do you think you are more of a *follower* of Jesus or a *lover* of Jesus?

2. I described myself as a "loved Son." Up to this point, how have you described yourself?

3. Do you see or believe that God is smiling at you? Why or why not?

———⎃———

_____

_____

_____

_____

_____

_____

_____

_____

_____

_____

_____

_____

_____

_____

_____

_____

_____

_____